FISHERMAN TO FOLLOWER:

THE LIFE AND TEACHING OF SIMON PETER

COMPILED BY HAYES PRESS

Copyright © Hayes Press 2015

All rights reserved. No part of this book may be reproduced, stored in a retrieval system, or transmitted in any form, without the written permission of Hayes Press.

Published by:

HAYES PRESS Publisher, Resources & Media,

The Barn, Flaxlands

Royal Wootton Bassett

Swindon, SN4 8DY

United Kingdom

www.hayespress.org

Unless otherwise indicated, all Scripture quotations are from the HOLY BIBLE, the New King James Version® (NKJV®). Copyright © 1982 Thomas Nelson, Inc. Used by permission. All rights reserved. Scriptures marked NIV are from New International Version®, NIV® Copyright © 1973, 1978, 1984, 2011 by Biblica, Inc.™ Used by permission. All rights reserved worldwide. Scriptures marked NASB are from the New American Standard Bible®, Copyright © 1960, 1962, 1963, 1968, 1971, 1972, 1973, 1975, 1977, 1995 by The Lockman Foundation. Used by permission. (www.Lockman.org)

If you enjoy reading this book and/or others by Hayes Press, we would really appreciate it if you could just take a couple of minutes to leave a brief review where you purchased his book.

CHAPTER ONE: THE CALL TO FOLLOW

It is said that Michelangelo took the pieces of stone that other people had rejected and put them to one side for his own use. He could see potential in these cast-offs that others had never visualized. The Lord approached Peter and made two statements to him. "You are Simon ... you shall be called Cephas" (John 1:42). It was not often that Peter was quiet. However, on this occasion, he never spoke a word. Quiet acquiescence wasn't one of his strengths. But although he may already have been aware of his innate weaknesses, his impetuous nature, his outspokenness, the fickleness which saw him blow hot with impulse, but cold as the snows of Lebanon, and his shaly, Simon-tendencies, he did not protest when the Lord spoke in glowing terms of what he would be as bed-rock Peter. When Scripture records that "Jesus looked at" Peter, it means that he looked intensely through him (John 1:42). The Lord did not ask Peter for his Curriculum Vitae, nor did He concern Himself with testimonials. The Lord didn't need witness from anyone, for He Himself knew what was in a man (John 2:25). He knew Simon Peter better than he knew himself. He looked through him, through the failures, to the time when Peter would act with rock-like dependability. He knew too, that before that was achieved there were some hard lessons for Simon to learn.

Deeply impressed by the Lord's perceptive promise, Simon Peter joined Andrew and, in all probability, John and James, in the company of "the Messiah" (John 1:41). The next day, two more, Philip and Nathaniel, were added to the little group. "And so" wrote Dr. Luxmoore, "there were perhaps half a dozen disciples with the Lord when He went down to Cana of Galilee". There, Peter, with the others, saw the Lord's first manifestation of His glory when "the simple wedding Guest" did to water what only almighty God can do, and turned it instantly into wine. It would surely have served to strengthen Peter's faith in the Lord's capability to replace dire deficiencies ("They have no wine") with overwhelming provision. John records the impact of "this beginning of signs" when Jesus "manifested His glory: and His disciples believed in Him" (2:11). The word "believed" implies that they put their trust in Him, especially for their spiritual well-being.

"Why", continued Dr. Luxmoore, "they ever went away again we may well marvel. We may also marvel why after the Lord has had us with Him for a precious and fruitful time He has again to come and find us occupied with everything else and again say, Follow Me". That they did go away is evident from Matthew 4:18-22, when the Lord found Simon and Andrew fishing. Had the Lord been mistaken? Was this man, Peter, demonstrating the sort of dependability that would repay the Lord's early faith in his rock-like qualities? Graciously, the Lord appealed to them, "Follow Me, and I will make you fishers of men" (Matthew 4:19). Peter's response was immediate. This, then, was the secret. "I will make you ..." The transformation was to be achieved in the Lord's company and by the divine hand that had forsaken forever the shaping of wood for the village folk of Nazareth for the moulding of lives that would soon turn "the world upside down" (Acts 17:6).

In this manner, in the days of Scripture, and today, the Lord approaches the most unlikely of people (1 Corinthians 1:26-28) with promises of victory. The marauding bands of Midianites and Amalekites, which had been destroying Israel's crops and cattle (Judges 6:4), forced Gideon to abandon the more usual threshing-sledge on an exposed site for the flail, or rod, in the smaller, sheltered winepress of Ophrah. His was a small, secretive service, hiding wheat from the enemy, not heading warriors in open conflict. Though perplexed and protesting, he was given the divine commission. "Go and ... save Israel", and the assurance of the divine Companion, "Surely I will be with you" (Judges 6:14-16). It is to just those kind of people, conscious of their own weakness, that God grants the needed grace for glorious victory (2 Corinthians 12:9,10). So Gideon was taken from beating out wheat in secret, through fear, to subduing kingdoms, through faith (Hebrews 11.32,33)! At Bethabara (the place of transition) the Lord took one man, Gideon, to replace his flail with a sword, and another, Peter, to replace his fish with souls! (Judges 7:24; John 1:28). Perhaps today, even as you read, the Lord is calling you to richer, more challenging service. This meditation could be your Bethabara, place of transition. But there are conditions attached.

Peter had been brought to Jesus (John 1:42). Next would come the call to go after Him (Mark 1:17). If Peter were to fulfil the potential that the Lord saw in him, then it would mean following. It was to cost Peter everything; his boat, his business, his nets and his family (Luke 5:11; 18:28), but the Lord would be true to His promise to return all that he had forfeited with unparalleled interest (Luke 18:29,30). If Peter sacrificed the thrill of coming to land with heavy draughts of fish, he secured the prospect of a glorious abundance on reaching the shores of the eternal kingdom of his Lord and Saviour (2 Peter 1:11).

"We lose what on ourselves we spend,

We have as treasures without end

Whatever, Lord, to Thee we lend,

Who givest all."

Both Peter and Gideon must have marvelled that the Lord had worked in them far beyond their highest expectations. He is still able "to do exceedingly abundantly above all that we think" (Ephesians 3:20). Disciple, the same Prospector, the Lord Jesus Christ, invites you, "Come ... after Me, and I will make you ..."

"I heard His call,

Come, follow.

That was all.

My gold grew dim,

My soul went after Him."

Who would not follow if they heard Him call?

"To" Jesus, "after" Him, and now, "with" Him (Mark 3:14). What a wealth of glorious experience is contained in those prepositions! Peter never forgot those rich periods of his life. They moulded his actions, his teaching and his character. Years later, he recalled for his readers, "We were with Him" (2 Peter 1:18). Timothy's years with Paul (Acts 16:3) were golden seams of informative training (2 Timothy 3:10), but they could not equal the first-hand privilege which Peter enjoyed as he walked and talked with the Master Himself. Inevitably, it showed, even though at times Peter wished that it didn't. "This man was also with Him" one of the servant girls said confidently (Luke 22:56). On a later, happier occasion, the religious leaders recognized the same undeniable fact that he "had been with Jesus" (Acts 4:13). It is bound to happen. Although he did not know it, Moses' face shone as a result of his being in the presence of God Exodus 34:29). It will happen to us, too, if we are prepared to submit our lives in unclouded exposure to the glorious Person of the Lord Jesus Christ. In the secret of His presence, the Lord the Spirit will transform these lacklustre lives of ours until they radiate the glory of the Lord (2 Corinthians 3:18).

"Take time to be holy, the world rushes on;

Spend much time in secret with Jesus alone.

By looking to Jesus, like Him thou shalt be;

Thy friends in thy conduct His likeness shall see"

Not only was Peter's life affected, but so was his teaching. "Blessed are those who are persecuted for righteousness' sake", the Lord taught him (Matthew 5:10). "If you should suffer for righteousness' sake, you are blessed", Peter wrote to the dispersed pilgrims (1 Peter 3:14). "Blessed are you when they revile and persecute you, and say all kinds of evil against you falsely for My sake", taught the Master (Matthew 5:11). "If you are reproached for the Name of Christ, blessed are you", echoed the servant (1 Peter 4:14). "Rejoice to the extent that you partake of Christ's sufferings", counselled Peter (1 Peter 4:13).

Hadn't he learned that too, from his Mentor on the mountain? "Rejoice and be exceeding glad, for great is your reward in heaven, for so they persecuted the prophets" (Matthew 5:12). Followers of the Man whose doing and teaching were perfectly harmonized (Acts 1:1) will also find, like Peter, that their life and lips tell the same unmistakable truth that they have "been with Jesus". Could there be a finer, more challenging contemplation than this, "that the life of Jesus also may be manifested in our body"? (2 Corinthians 4:10). Shall we not say of our Lord, "He must increase, but I must decrease" (John 3:30)?

"Higher than the highest heavens,

Deeper than the deepest sea,

Lord, Thy love at last hath conquered,

Grant me now my soul's petition,

None of self, and all of Thee."

"And when He had called His twelve disciples to Him ... these twelve Jesus sent out" (Matthew 10:1,5). To Him, after Him, with Him, and now, sent out for Him. Though the mission of the twelve was a special apostolic work, the same sequence must characterize all the Lord's servants. He is using the hours of secret communion to shape us for His commission, "Go" (Matthew 28:19). Today, the challenge is to the same progression. The Lord is seeking those who will spend time with Him before He can send them out for Him.

"So send I you - to leave your life's ambitions,

To die to dear desire, self-will resign,

To labour long and love where men revile you,

So send I you - to lose your life in Mine."

CHAPTER TWO: TWO CATCHES OF FISH

Some men are melted and moulded in one flash of brilliance from the Throne of Heaven, as was Paul on the dusty highway to Damascus; other men are chiselled out with the Master Sculptor's tools from the rough granite, as was Peter the Rockman. The great Worker (John 5:17) chooses His own methods and materials. Some may reply as Moses did, "Oh Lord, I am not eloquent" (Exodus 4:10), or as Isaiah, "I am undone ... I am a man of unclean lips" (Isaiah 6:5), or as Jeremiah, "Ah, Lord God! behold, I cannot speak: for I am a child" (Jeremiah 1:6), or as Gideon, "Oh Lord, wherewith shall I save Israel? Behold, my family is the poorest ... and I am the least" (Judges 6:15 RV), or as blinded Saul, "Who art Thou, Lord?" (Acts 9:5 RV), or as impetuous Peter, "Depart from me; for I am a sinful man, O Lord" (Luke 5:8).

God, desiring workers in His service, puts no hindrance in the way. Rather He uses that which lies to our hand. Of Moses He asks, "What is that in thine hand? ... A rod." He took David from the sheepfolds to feed His people ... "so he fed them according to the integrity of his heart; and guided them by the skilfulness of his hands" (Psalm 78:70-72 RV). Paul was a tent-maker, and tabernacles and sanctuaries are very evident in his teaching (see Acts 17:24; Ephesians 2:21; Hebrews 9, etc.). Peter was a fisher of fish, called to be a fisher of men (Luke 5:1-11).

We should ponder well these scenes by the Sea of Galilee, that first scene at the call to higher service (Luke 5.1-11; Matthew 4:18-22; Mark 1:16-20), and that last scene recorded only by John (John 21). Why was this scene re-enacted? The same rod that became a serpent at the beginning of Moses' career was stretched across the waters of the Red Sea. There is a significance in God's repetitions (compare Job 33:14, 29-80).

Peter was a skilled fisherman, and although he had caught nothing on those two notable occasions, the "washing" and "mending" of nets suggest that they had previously been successfully used; and Peter is commissioned by the Lord Himself to "cast a hook and take a fish," on the other occasion where we read of his following his original craft after his call (Matthew 17:24, 25). He could catch with net and with line. It is not the aspect of the hunter here. Jeremiah, in chapter 16:16, foretells a day when God will send fishers first to fish His people, then afterwards, hunters to hunt them. These crafts are so different. The former needs art and skill and patience to catch alive and not bruise in the catching, the latter, force and violence and rush, with no concern in overdriving even those with young. We need to cultivate the former.

We take ourselves, in thought, to those shores of Galilee of the nations (Isaiah 9) to look upon the pressing multitudes (Luke 5), hungering for the word of God. Into the frail, unoccupied, and borrowed boat the Master steps, and condescendingly asks its owner Simon, to come in beside Him, and to row Him out a little from the shore. Then "He said unto Simon ... let down your nets for a draught." Simon answered, "At Thy word I will let down the nets." And the Master of oceans, and earth, and skies brought from their home in the deep a great multitude of fishes to those nets. Here indeed was the Creator, the last Adam, with full control over "the fish of the sea, (and) whatsoever passeth through the paths of the seas" (Psalm 8 RV).

Then there arose a need for more fishers. This is the Lord's order. He will supply the men for the work. Peter can bear up no longer, and, at Jesus' knees he cries, "Depart from me, for I am a sinful man, O Lord." When a man realizes his own sinfulness and weakness in relation to God's holiness and power, God may use him, and the outshining of His glory does not repel, but rather attracts the willing penitent to Himself. "FEAR NOT" is the word, so often repeated in the past (Isaiah 41:10,14; 43:1,5; 44:2,8; 54:4; Daniel 10.12; etc.). "From henceforth" - a complete change in character – you will be catching men alive - a continuous occupation, catching men for life, and not for death, taking them from the troubled seas to the new atmosphere of the kingdom of the Son of His love.

Mark tells us what they left for this new vocation; their father, their boats, their hired servants, their catch, their all. We long for those scenes to be re-enacted in our day, for filled nets. Many days pass by, many lessons are taught and learned, a few more hammer strokes are needed on Cephas, and again we take ourselves to the shores of Galilee. Peter is in good company with Nathanael, who had confessed, "Rabbi, Thou art the Son of God; Thou art King of Israel" (John 1:49 RV); and with Thomas, who had made a belated confession, "My Lord and my God" (John 20:28). John also was there, and he has left us such a record as proves that Jesus is the Christ, the Son of God (John 20:81). Peter, too, had earlier declared, by divine inspiration, "Thou art the Christ, the Son of the living God" (Matthew 16:16 RV). Yet how often in John 21 Peter is called "Simon Peter," his old and his new natures still combined. And how significant it is for the Lord Himself to repeat, three times, "Simon, son of John," as if to say, "Where is that rocklike character I once conferred on you, in the name Peter?"

The significant differences between the latter and the former catches of fish are noteworthy. Firstly, we observe that both events were prefaced by a futile night's work in their mundane occupation. This is by no means an infrequent occurrence in our own experiences. But John 21 presents a resurrection scene, the "day was now breaking, Jesus stood on the beach." He is not with them on the waters; He was standing on the beach, but He is intensely interested in their work and well-being, for He asks, "Children, have ye aught to eat? They answered Him, No. And He said unto them, Cast the net on the right side of the boat, and ye shall find." There is no breaking net in this scene - no schisms (the meaning of the Greek word used). The catch was taken into the boat in the earlier scene, here it is hauled ashore. The catch was innumerable on the first occasion, here it is definitely numbered, for it is a divine prerogative to number, measure or weigh, and all the fish are "great."

So together they feast with Him, the Risen Lord, on the shore of the sea of their many trials. But men must be pliable in His service. The keen "fisher" may yet have to be a patient "shepherd", feeding lambs, tending yearlings, feeding sheep. Thus it was a sure seal to Peter that his thrice-repeated denial had been forgiven, when the Chief Shepherd put into his care His own beloved sheep. Peter remembered this scene in after years, when in his first epistle (chapter 5) he reminds the elders and fellow-shepherds of the flock of the Dispersion, of their Chief Shepherd's return and expectation; and he recalls the "girding" ... but ... "with humility."

Following this latter scene, and unquestionably linked with it, the Lord twice asks Peter if he desires Him by deliberate judgement and choice (Greek - agape; Latin - dilegere). Twice Peter repeats, "Thou knowest that I love Thee," otherwise translated, "Thou art the Object of my special attachment and personal affection" (Greek - phileo; Latin - amare). On the third occasion the Master asks deliberately, changing to Peter's own chosen word, "Lovest thou Me? "There is, in the thrice-repeated avowal of love by Peter, an allusion to his thrice-repeated denial. So, admitting the omniscience of his risen Lord, he exclaims,

"Thou knowest all things, Thou knowest that I love (phileo) Thee." Then is uttered that simple yet pregnant word, "Follow Thou Me" ... meanwhile the beloved apostle John follows unbidden!

CHAPTER THREE: IN THE STEPS OF THE MASTER

After the call of the disciples, early and lasting impressions leaving many treasured memories were fixed in Peter's mind as he companioned with Christ to such places as Capernaum, Nain, Bethsaida, Gennesaret, Phoenicia, Caesarea Philippi and Decapolis (ten cities). All of these were within reasonable walking distance of the Sea of Galilee and to this geographical area we now come in our present study of Peter in the steps of the Master. For about two years of His public ministry the Lord lived and taught in and around Galilee, located in the northern part of Israel. On the shores of the lake which he knew so well, Peter together with James and John, witnessed miracles, wonders and signs in such profusion that he must have been one of the most privileged men ever to have lived. All of this was accompanied by rich teaching including what we know as "the sermon on the mount" and "the kingdom parables". Would we not have loved to exchange places with Peter, even for a day?

Before focusing on two particular experiences, let us recall some of the amazing events Peter witnessed in these Galilean teaching tours of the Master, bearing in mind that each event strengthened his faith and revealed more of the glorious Person he was following. Take for example the case of the centurion's servant. This was a remarkable healing because it was done at a distance, an extra dimension which was an added marvel. Then there was the demoniac who may have been known to Peter. Perhaps as a curious boy he had sighted the madman and understood well the futile efforts of men to control him, but now the demoniac sat at the Master's feet and in his right mind. What can we say about the well documented feeding of the five thousand? This miracle was so public and extensive, involving so many people that it must have amazed Peter, especially as he was close at hand to see how the miracle actually happened. Thereafter as distributor and collector of leftovers he would be further confounded. When we read "great multitudes followed Him, and He healed them all" (Matthew 12:15), we can only speculate on the variety of miracles contained in this statement, but Peter, together with the others, must have been left in no doubt that the Person he was following had "come from God" as Nicodemus said.

What a wealth of teaching, especially about the Lord Himself, accompanied these miracles. Lord of the Sabbath, Forgiver of sins, to name but two, so that ultimately he must have shared the same sentiments as others who said, "never man spoke like this Man". There were a few special experiences Peter was privileged to share with James and John. One of them was the raising of Jairus' daughter. Beyond controversy the local people, and most importantly the family, all considered the girl to be dead. Funeral arrangements were under way without delay as is common in the east. The mourners had started their wailing and the flute players were in readiness. Jesus said, "she is not dead, but sleeping" (Luke 8:52), and although it is debatable what Jesus actually meant, there is no doubt it was a stunning miracle and the parents were astonished. Peter saw the effect on the family at close quarters and must have shared in their astonishment. Looking over these Galilean years we see that there was a vast weight of evidence now underpinning Peter's faith, that the One he was following was indeed "the Christ, the Son of the living God".

This Galilean ministry could hardly be passed over without a reference to Peter's own special experience on the lake. How many times as a child or even as a fisherman he had fallen in we cannot know, but this time it was going to be different. He had seen the figure on the water and heard Him say, "It is I; do not be afraid" (Matthew 14:27). Then, quick as ever, he responded, "Lord, if it is You, command me to come to You on the water". "Come", Jesus said, and over the side of the boat went Peter. What must it have been for a fisherman of Galilee to walk on waves? Then there is failure and it seems to have come so quickly: Peter is sinking in the stormy sea, but the Lord is at hand rescuing Peter as He would again and again rescue the failing disciple.

The early chapters of the book of the Acts contain considerable narrative about Peter, and there we find him firm as a rock, with all boldness testifying for his Lord and Master. Fearless in his preaching, working miracles and leading the disciples in evangelism. It was Peter also who was spokesman for the apostles when Ananias and Saphira were condemned. Prison and beatings awaited him. It is clear therefore that Peter had been moulded into a true, faithful and fearless disciple of his Master and much of this must have been the result of those Galilean travels, the memory of which kept him close to the Lord in those early difficult days of the New Covenant churches of God.

Peter's character as a bondservant, developed so fully after Pentecost, was moulded on the servant character of Christ. This was often seen in the Lord's dealings with men and events, such as the feeding of the five thousand, in which the Saviour saw the multitudes as sheep not having a shepherd. These events must have left indelible impressions on Peter's mind and influenced his behaviour in later years. Although he became a forceful leader there was no incompatibility between this and being at the same time a humble slave. "I am among you as the One who serves", the Lord said (Luke 22:27), and this must also be true of us today, serving each other in addition to serving the same Master as Peter.

What an encouragement all this is for disciples of our Lord Jesus Christ. In his second letter Peter describes his readers as those with a like precious faith and we like them share that same faith in our Saviour. We have received divine power (2 Peter 1:3) that we might be partakers of the divine nature, especially as it is to be seen in our godly living and behaviour: so we add to our faith virtue, knowledge, self-control, patience, godliness, brotherly kindness and love. What does all this produce? "You will never stumble," Peter writes (2 Peter 1:10). All of this is strong encouragement indeed since it comes from a disciple who stumbled several times himself after having failed (see Matthew 26 verse 33).

Sometimes we experience that sinking feeling as the waves of difficulty, adversity and lack of trust in the Saviour overtake us. How good to know that He is immediately beside us with an outstretched hand. Then all we have to do is to stretch out in faith and He will lift us up in safety so that we can be with our fellow disciples again and more importantly know that the Master also is with us. Peter who himself walked in the steps of the Master, has one final message for us. "Follow His steps: who committed no sin, nor was guile found in His mouth" (1 Peter 2:21-22), and "grow in the grace and knowledge of our Lord and Saviour Jesus Christ" (2 Peter 3:18).

CHAPTER FOUR: REVELATION AND REBUKE

It is no doubt the experience of all disciples of the Lord Jesus Christ who are zealous to follow the Master, that at times we are good examples of what we should be, and at other times we are not! Such was also the experience of the apostle Peter. To him the Lord said: "Blessed are you, Simon Barjona, because flesh and blood did not reveal this to you, but My Father who is in heaven" (Matthew 16:17), and a very short time later also: "Get behind Me, Satan! You are a stumbling block to Me; for you are not setting your mind on God's interests, but man's". On the first occasion Peter was giving expression to the great truth of the deity of the Son of the living God; on the second occasion rebuking the Lord for telling of His future suffering, death and resurrection. Understanding so much, yet understanding so little! It is ever so when feeble men seek to appreciate the majesty of Deity. The more we learn about Him, the more we appreciate how little we know Him and love Him.

Luke tells us that it was while the Lord Jesus was praying that He questioned the disciples about who men said that He was. They were at Caesarea Philippi, at one of the sources of the Jordan River, the river that brings the water of life to so much of Israel. What an appropriate place for the One who was the origin of "living water" to question those who would soon take His message to the world. "Who do people say that the Son of Man is?" When the Lord asks a question, it is not because He does not know the answer, but to teach the one He questions, and us. But the crucial question then and now is: "But who do you say that I am?" Each person must answer that question. And Peter stated the divinely revealed truth simply and clearly, "Thou art the Christ, the Son of the living God". He is the anointed One, the Messiah, in whom "all the fulness of Deity dwells in bodily form" (Colossians 2:9). He is God, the Son. The Lord asked about Himself as the Son of Man, a position to which He had stooped so very low; sadly, most only thought of Him as some man's son! But Peter knew that this Son of Man was none other than the Son of God. How was he so sure? He later declared, "... we were eyewitnesses of His majesty" (2 Peter 1:16).

He had certainly already seen the sick raised to health, even his own mother-in-law (Matthew 8:15); he had seen the mighty works in the blind receiving sight, the lepers cleansed, the deaf hearing, the dead being raised up (Matthew 11:5); he had seen the Lord walking on water and had ventured towards Him on the stormy seas; he had witnessed the wind cease the moment the Lord entered the boat and had proclaimed then with the others in the boat, "You are certainly God's Son" (Matthew 14:33). But there was more to his conviction than just the things that he had witnessed, amazing though they were. God the Father had revealed this wonderful truth to him directly and personally. If there had been any doubt before, there was none now. "Blessed are you, Simon Barjona ..." You have had the Word of God communicated directly to you; you have had the Word of God illuminated before you; and you have received it by faith. There is no other way to receive God's Word!

All who believe in the Lord Jesus, "this Rock" whom God smote, are built by Him into what He calls "My Church" in Matthew 16:18. How very personal! And it is a Church so intimately associated with Him as its Head that it is known as "the Church, which is His Body" (Ephesians 1:22,23). Peter was to learn more of this Church on the day of Pentecost when

Christ would begin building it, having said at Caesarea Philippi, "I will build My Church".

The Church, the Body, comprising all believers since Pentecost, is one over which the gates of Hades have no power (W.E. Vine, in his Expository Dictionary of New Testament Words, states: "The importance and strength of gates made them viewed as synonymous with power. By metonymy, the gates stood for those who held government and administered justice there"). The gates of Hades (the place of dead ones) cannot rob this Church of its members; Christ, who is the Rock on which it stands and by whom it is built, has justly met and extinguished the power in these gates, so that they can have no power over the Church.

It is as a result of that divine revelation Peter was given the keys of the kingdom of heaven, authority from the hand of the One who has all authority, and went out to the world and preached about the Christ, the Son of the living God. "Therefore let all the house of Israel know for certain that God has made Him both Lord and Christ - this Jesus whom you crucified" (Acts 2:36). Had he not been absolutely convinced of this Man's identity, and the authority by which he spoke about Him, he could not have been an instrument of service in the divine Builder's hand.

Those who accepted the message, and were thereby built by the Lord into this Body of believers, were loosed from sin, while others who rejected the message were bound in their sin. The tense of the verb indicates that the binding occurred in heaven before it ever occurred on earth: "and whatever you shall bind on earth shall be [having been] bound in heaven, and whatever you shall loose on earth shall be [having been] loosed in heaven" (Matthew 16:19). Peter did not determine who was bound or loosed. But he confirmed what God in heaven had done: in revealing the truth of the gospel. And he knew it was so because he knew the One of whom he spoke was none other than the Christ, the Son of the living God. "What God has cleansed, no longer consider unholy" (Acts 10:15). You bind what has been bound, and you loose what has been loosed. You have the keys of the authority of the Lord to do so.

Peter may well have thought that the kingdom of God was upon them, that this was the time when the Lord was going to restore it to Israel (Luke 19:11; see also Acts 1:6 where the actual question was asked). Here was the Anointed One; He was here to build; the gates of Hades were ineffective against His building; He had given Peter the keys and binding authority! What excitement! What a mountaintop experience! What a time to be alive! What a shock then when the Christ of God "began to show His disciples that He must go to Jerusalem, and suffer many things from the elders and chief priests and scribes, and be killed, and be raised up on the third day" (Matthew 16:21). Peter's hopes were dashed. He was indignant and took the Lord aside to correct Him:

"God forbid it, Lord! This shall never happen to You". How can this happen to the Christ the Son of God? The Lord's response indicates however that this was not simply Peter's impetuous nature. There was a more significant battle going on, and it involved Satan, the enemy of God, the tempting Devil, ever on the prowl to destroy the work of Christ if possible. But, as it was impossible in the wilderness, so also now: "Get behind Me, Satan! You are a stumbling block to Me; for you are not setting your mind on God's interests, but man's". Peter's interest was that the Son of God should set up His kingdom now, and that he was going to be involved in it. Satan was interested in that too, for that would do away with the Cross by which he would be rendered powerless. What is God's interest? "God our Saviour desires all men to be saved and to come to the knowledge of the truth" (1 Timothy 2:3,4). The suffering must come, the Cross must come, the tomb must come, and the Christ must be raised, for ever victorious over sin, death and the evil one, and be seated "at the right hand of the Majesty on high" (Hebrews 1:3).

In the hours and days after the Lord's death, closeted behind locked doors for fear of the Jews, the disciples would begin to remember the words of the Lord. When it was announced to them that He was raised, and then when He appeared to them, and to Peter individually, and taught them, the whole thing made sense. And Peter, with the keys and with the message, went out to the world to preach about His Lord and Christ. What did he teach? He taught what the Lord had taught him. The disciple who wishes to go after the Lord must take up his own cross and follow Him. Some did that literally not many years afterwards, Peter included.

Indeed, Peter said to the Lord, "Behold, we have left everything and followed You" (Matthew 19:27). They'd left their families and homes and businesses. How quickly then went back to the things they had left when they forsook Him and fled on the night of His betrayal! But Peter repented and was able to teach the way of the disciple as the way of the Cross, that those who would be His disciples must deny themselves, and follow Him: follow Him through the waters of baptism; follow Him to the place where His authority as Son over God's house is exercised; follow Him in spirit to the place where He performs the duties of High Priest; follow Him in a lifestyle that is "worthy of the calling with which you have been called" (Ephesians 4:1), "worthy of the gospel of Christ" (Philippians 1:27, and "worthy of the Lord, to please Him in all respects" (Colossians 1:10). He is the Christ, the Son of the living God. When He commands,

His authority is absolute. And we who love Him must obey Him!

CHAPTER FIVE: UPON THIS ROCK?

All the acts of the Lord are important and full of significance, for upon the works and words of the Lord would rest, as upon a foundation, the teachings of the Faith. After the memorable night which Andrew and the other disciple (presumably John) spent with the Lord, as recorded in John 1, Andrew set off to find his brother Peter and to bring him to Jesus. When the Lord looked on him, He said, "Thou art Simon the son of John: thou shalt be called Cephas (which is by interpretation Peter)." Peter means, as the Revised Version Margin shows, Rock or Stone.

Petros, the Greek word for Peter, is derived from Petra, which Liddell and Scott say means a rock, such as stands out in the sea or on a beach, a ledge or shelf of rock, or a rocky peak or ridge. Who can doubt that this change in Simon's name to Peter had further things in view, as we connect John 1:42 with Matthew 16:18-20? The Lord refers back to the time of John 1 when He speaks of Peter's confession: "Thou art the Christ, the Son of the living God." When Andrew found his brother Simon he said to him, "We have found the Messiah (which is, being interpreted, Christ)." But Peter's knowledge of who Jesus was did not rest merely on Andrew's words; there was a divine revelation to Peter then, of which the Lord said, "Blessed art thou, Simon Bar-jonah: for flesh and blood hath not revealed it unto thee', but My Father which is in heaven." It was this revelation that so changed Peter that the Lord renamed him. Simon was his natural name, the name of the son of a fisherman of Galilee, who was also himself a fisherman, but Peter is his name according to grace, of him who had the glorious revelation of who Jesus of Nazareth is, which made him a blessed or happy man for ever.

Then the Lord adds, "And I also say unto thee, that thou art Peter (Petros), and upon this Rock (Petra) I will build My Church; and the gates of Hades (hell) shall not prevail against it." Here is a further revelation. The first and preeminent truth to be revealed to man is certainly connected with the Divine Being, to know the Son and the Father, and also the Eternal Spirit by whom all revelation of God is made. Then follows on Church truth, as here, and in connection with this Church is the eternal security of all believers in Christ in this dispensation, for against this Church, in which all believers are since Pentecost (Acts 2), hell's gates cannot prevail.

The devil has always sought to corrupt and destroy the precious truth of God. He cannot destroy the truth itself, thank God! But he can corrupt men's understanding of it. We know something of the corruptions of the church of Rome in regard to this verse (Matthew 16:18), in that they say that Peter is the Rock (Petros, a piece of rock is, according to them, Petra, the Rock itself). Then as to what the Lord calls "My Church" that, they say, is the church of Rome, and they point to its continuance from apostolic times as the proof that the gates of hell have not prevailed against it. The same of course could be said of the Greek church, the Coptic church, the Armenian church, as of the Roman church, if continuance in time is what is meant by the gates of hell not prevailing against it.

Then, as Peter is the Rock, in their view, and being the first bishop of Rome, which he was not, his seat and see have been occupied in a continuous succession since Peter's time. Alas for Rome, history will not bear out a pure unbroken succession, and perhaps worse still, some of the bishops of Rome were most wicked, immoral men. But such men, they say, were Christ's vicars on earth. Such are the corruptions of the devil.

The word "church" is first used in the New Testament in Matthew 18.18, and it is important to note the meaning and connection in which a word is first used, for, generally speaking, it sheds light on its use afterwards in Scripture. The word for church in the Greek means "to call out," and signifies a "called-out people." It is applied to the people of Israel, gathered together in the wilderness, who had been called out by God from Egypt (Acts 7:38; Hosea 11:1).

Here in Matthew 16:18 is a called-out people by Christ, for He calls it "My Church." What call is it that these people heard and responded to? This we shall find in Matthew 11:28: "Come unto Me, all ye that labour and are heavy laden, and I will give you rest." All who feel the insupportable burden of sin upon a convicted heart, and who labour in vain to obtain rest by personal effort, are invited to come to the blessed and only Rest-giver, the Son of the Father referred to in this passage. See Matthew 11.27. Was not His lament in John 5:40, "Ye will not come to Me, that ye may have life"? He gave the people of Capernaum the assurance, and many others since, "Him that cometh to Me I will in no wise cast out" (John 6:37).

Upon what Rock did the Son of God intend to build His Church? Upon Peter (Petros, a piece of rock) or upon Petra, the Rock? The answer of every sincere heart must be, not upon Petros but upon Petra. The Greek of this verse (Matthew 16:18) is as the English translation: "And I also to thee say, that thou art Peter (Petros), and upon this the Rock (Petra) I will build My Church" (literally, "of Me the Church"). "This the Rock" points back to what Peter had confessed – "Thou art the Christ, the Son of the living God." It would have been blasphemy to a true Israelite to have called a mere man, such as Peter, "the Rock."

The Rock to the Israelite was Jehovah, who asked in Isaiah 44:8, "Is there a God beside Me? Yea, there is no Rock, I know not any." "The Rock was Christ" (1 Corinthians 10:4).

In contrast to the Rock in Matthew 16:18, we have Peter speaking of the Lord as the living Stone, in 1 Peter 2:8-7. Here he uses the Greek word "lithos". One of the words for rock in Hebrew means "a cliff", which is similar in meaning to the Greek for Rock. Stone (lithos) in 1 Peter 2 means building stone or stone dressed suitably for building. In Matthew 16, both Petros (Peter) and Petra (Christ, the Rock) stand related to the truth of the Church which is His (Christ's) Body (Ephesians 1:22, 28), which is "My Church" of Matthew 16:18.

But Christ, the living Stone, was laid in the heavenly Zion as a sure foundation, and will in due time be laid in Zion, at Jerusalem, in the Holy Land, when He comes again (Isaiah 28:16). He and those who have come to Him (not as Saviour, as in Matthew 11.28, but as the rejected One, rejected by men) are viewed as living stones and are seen as God's spiritual house, which is God's house for this dispensation. Christ the Rock and Christ the Stone are associated with different truths; the former is the foundation on which the Church which is Christ's Body is built, the living Stone is the foundation of God's house, upon which each several church of God is built. Paul says that as a wise master builder He laid a foundation and another builds on it. This foundation, and there can be no other, is Jesus Christ. See 1 Corinthians 3:10, 11. Paul laid the same foundation in connection with the planting of the church of God in Corinth as God had laid in Zion, but he never laid Christ the Rock, nor has any man built one soul into the Church which is Christ's Body, on Christ the Rock; that is the work of Christ Himself exclusively.

CHAPTER SIX: EYEWITNESSES OF HIS MAJESTY

Dream up a fabulous world, invent some fantastic characters, weave an imaginary story line around them, and you have a myth in the making. Libraries, bookshops and our childhood memories are full of them. Religion and cults have developed similarly, and have deceived many by their imagination appeal. No matter how attractive or plausible they may be on the surface, they are but "cunningly devised fables" (2 Peter 1:16). Not so the apostle Peter's testimony of what he saw when, accompanied by James and John, two of his fellow apostles, he went with Jesus up into a mountain to pray. Peter later wrote of the event in 2 Peter 1:1&18, declaring "we were eyewitnesses". What happened was neither myth nor dream. It was not a "cunningly devised fable" for an impressionable audience. Peter's own testimony is supported by the Gospel accounts. Please read Matthew 17:1-8, Mark 9:2-8 and Luke 9:28-36.

Isn't Luke 9:36 a most amazing detail? "And they held their peace, and told no man in those days any of the things which they had seen". Held their peace! How could they have bottled it up? They must have been longing to tell the world. Of course, the Lord had commanded them to say nothing (Mark 9:9). We cannot imagine what it would have been like to see the Lord's face day after day during His life on earth. But to have seen Him transfigured before us in majestic glory would surely have changed our whole perspective on life forever.

Peter was spiritually alert. Before the transfiguration, the Lord asked the disciples, "But who say ye that I am?" (Matthew 16:15), and Peter uttered the remarkable answer revealed to him by God, "Thou art the Christ, the Son of the Living God". A few breaths later, however, he began to "rebuke" the Lord for speaking of suffering, rejection and death. What boldness! Rebuking the Christ! Clearly he had not understood what He had said, for it was Satan, not Peter, whom the Lord in turn rebuked, "Get thee behind Me, Satan" (Matthew 16:23). What a man of contrasts Peter was! He had perceived by the Spirit of God that Jesus was the Christ, but it was still hidden from him that the Christ had to "suffer these things" (Luke 24:26). He knew nothing of the looming Cross of Calvary.

The day never to be forgotten arrived, and the Lord Jesus led the three fishermen up into the mountain, where they would be quite alone. Why no Andrew, nor any other disciples to see this marvellous sight? What a privilege to be chosen! The testimonies of these men would stand the test of time, confirming each other, as do the three Gospel accounts. "A threefold cord is not quickly broken" (Ecclesiastes 4:12).

They reached the allotted place. As they prayed, the Lord Jesus was transfigured before them. He was changed before their very eyes, and His outward human appearance instantly revealed the radiant glory of His deity. Such divine glory is His by right and by nature, for as the only begotten Son of the Father He is co-equal with His Father in deity (John 1:1), honour (John 5:23) and glory (John 17:5; Hebrews 1:3).

Three distinct changes to the Lord during His transfiguration are described.

1. His face "did shine as the sun" (Matthew 17:2).

2. His garments: "became white as the light" (Matthew 17:2), "became glistering, exceeding white"

(Mark 9:3) and "became white and dazzling" (Luke 9:29).

3. The fashion of His countenance "was altered" (Luke 9:29).

Only Luke reveals that the Lord's face changed, as well as shining as the sun, and His garments becoming dazzlingly white. We cannot say how it was changed. Perhaps it became more akin to the divine face which John saw while in the Spirit on Patmos (Revelation 1:16) than the earthly face of Him who had "no beauty that we should desire Him" (Isaiah 53:2).

The disciples had been drowsy, tired with the ascent no doubt, but when the transfiguration occurred, they were wide awake (Luke 9:32). Peter and his companions saw the glory of the transfigured Jesus. They gazed upon Him and could even withstand the brilliance of His face. They did not cast themselves down, nor cover their eyes although full of awe-inspired fear. Peter's memory was completely unclouded even years later when he wrote, "we were eyewitnesses of His majesty" (2 Peter 1:16).

Clearly they saw the glorious Lord with Moses and Elijah. It almost presents a picture of small children sitting at their parents' feet as the parents talk of matters beyond the children's understanding, and yet the children gaze upwards in wonder. The Lord was speaking of "His decease which He was about to accomplish at Jerusalem" (Luke 9:31). Peter did not appreciate the significance of this momentous discussion. He still had not grasped the meaning of the Lord's "decease", one thing he knew, "Rabbi, it is good for us to be here" (Mark 9:5). His heart was surely overcome with awe at the unimaginable scene, and whatever fear he felt in the presence of such glory, there was no better place to be at that moment. What was more, he was prepared to say so.

What about us? How quickly our conversation becomes mundane after we have been in the Lord's presence. Let us be more concerned about saying to each other at the end of our worship, "It was good". Next, the bright cloud enveloped them and a voice spoke. When Moses and the children of Israel stood at the foot of Mount Sinai and the Lord descended in a thick cloud, even Moses was full of fear (Exodus 19:16-19). When the Lord spoke, "they that heard intreated that no word more be spoken unto them" (Hebrews 12:19).

The mount of transfiguration was entirely different, for the transfigured Son of Man was present, and God was pleased to speak to the three men, "This is My Beloved Son, in whom I am well pleased; hear ye Him" (Matthew 17:5). The voice of God confirmed that this glorious Person was none other than the Holy One of God. Even Moses and Elijah, whom Peter recognized, were glorious in appearance, not of themselves, but because of the Lord's presence. After the voice had spoken, Peter's unthinking words concerning tabernacles are forgotten. No need for tabernacles, Peter, just look at your Master, He is none other than Jehovah, God the Son whom you walk beside day by day.

Again we cannot imagine what the sound of the voice was like for we have never heard such a voice with our human ears. Peter did, and he never forgot it. It affected him as powerfully as the sight of the Lord in His glory. His later testimony is completely convincing, "there came such a voice to Him from the excellent glory ... and this voice we ourselves heard come out of heaven" (2 Peter 1:17-18). On hearing it, the disciples "fell on their face, and were sore afraid" (Matthew 17:6).

Perhaps we should learn from this reaction of fear before the voice of God. The Scriptures teach us to be so moved by the Word of God, "but to this man will I look, even to him that trembleth at My Word" (Isaiah 66: 2). Do I, and do you, sometimes adopt a blase attitude to God's Word? Remember Peter and his friends, prostrate on the ground, and afterwards all they could see was "Jesus ... alone" (Luke 9:36). When we read the Scriptures, do we see "Jesus alone"? If not, is it because we have failed to fall on our face?

It is surely not by accident that on returning to the other disciples, and the three restraining themselves from describing the indescribable, as commanded by the Lord, the Holy Spirit brings before us the healing of the demon-possessed boy (Luke 9:38-43). One can only feel for the heartbreak of the father to see his little lad being convulsed with an evil spirit. The disciples could do nothing to heal him. Then the Lord Jesus rebuked the evil spirit, healed the boy and gave him back to his father. The reaction of the crowd is remarkable, "they were all astonished at the majesty of God" (v.43). The One whose majestic deity was seen in the mountain equally manifested His deity as Son of Man, by "doing good, and healing all that were oppressed of the Devil" (Acts 10:38).

The Holy Spirit is revealing that the deity of Christ on the mountain is no greater than the deity of Christ on the plain. Peter saw His glory, heard the voice and saw the demon-possessed boy healed. No wonder that after the Lord's ascension into heaven, he declared, "Jesus of Nazareth, a man approved of God" (Acts 2:22). A faithful witness, Peter was not deluded by fancies or legends. The things he witnessed influenced him profoundly, deepening his love for the Lord.

Shall we, who read his eyewitness report, not be similarly influenced? May the Spirit of God give us the same assurance of "the power and coming of our Lord Jesus Christ" (2 Peter 1:16), and touch our lives accordingly.

CHAPTER SEVEN: WHAT THEN SHALL WE HAVE?

The principle of reward runs right through the Scriptures. In Genesis 15, the Lord describes Himself to Abraham as his shield and his exceeding great reward. In Revelation 22:12 the Lord says, "Behold, I come quickly; and My reward is with Me, to render to each man according as his work is" - a lovely promise from a gracious Lord. To His own He couples with the assurance of His coming, the promise of reward. Against such a background Simon Peter's question in Matthew 19:27 might at first appear to be quite legitimate. "We have left all, and followed Thee; what then shall we have?" Peter had heard the Lord's conversation with the rich young man when treasure in heaven had been mentioned, a sequel to selling what he had, giving to the poor and following the Lord.

In His immediate reply to the question the Lord was very gracious. Never had it occurred to Peter that when he left all to follow Christ it would lead to a hundredfold reward, the inheritance of eternal life, and an association with the Son of Man in His glory; to sit on a throne and arbitrate in the affairs of Israel. We too, by heeding the gospel call to come to Christ and to follow Him, have entered into a sphere of untold blessing and glory. When we came as poor sinners to the Saviour we were little aware that in that moment of receiving Christ we were raised and seated with Him in heavenly places in Christ. Divine grace brought us to a realm of untold richness and glory, being placed in Christ to see His glory and to be eternally associated with Him. However, apart from His first gracious response, the Lord discerned that Peter was entering a life of discipleship and service from wrong motives. The question, "What then shall we have?" indicated a state of mind more concerned with receiving than giving, surely a wrong attitude with which to begin a life of service for the Lord, hence the parable in chapter 20 of the householder who hired labourers.

The Lord tells us of two distinct classes of labourers, the first who entered into an agreement with the householder and served for an agreed wage - a penny a day. The second class, embracing all who were appointed at the third hour, the sixth, the ninth and the eleventh hours, served on the householder's promise that he would give to them whatsoever was right. These men were content to serve, trusting the householder's word that they would receive at the end of the day that which was right; the interpretation of this was left to the householder.

Peter's question, "What then shall we have?" placed him in the category of those labourers who served with their terms and conditions of service spelled out: It showed that Peter was an immature believer, not understanding as yet the ways of his Lord or his own position. In 2 Peter 1:1, Peter describes himself as a servant (bondservant - a slave) of Jesus Christ. Peter has advanced here in his knowledge of the Lord and His ways and in his estimation of himself before the Lord. A slave has no entitlements; he is not in a position to ask for privileges or to make demands. He is dependent on the goodwill of his master for the bare necessities of life. All that a slave has is at the disposal of his master: his time, his strength and energy, every part of him is to be spent in the service of the One who bought him, with no expectation of reward in return.

"According to His promise, we look for new heavens and a new earth, wherein dwelleth righteousness" (2 Peter 3:13). We have no other guidance in this matter, we accept His Word, and resting on it look forward to better days and a better place to come. In the matter of reward we again rest on His word and promise. We have no other guidance and no claims on the Lord; we accept and rest on His word - "Behold, I come quickly; and My reward is with Me, to render to each man according as his work is" (Revelation 22:12), and again, "If any man's work shall abide ... he shall receive a reward" (1 Corinthians 3:14).

A consideration of such scriptures leads us to realize that there is, of course, a solemn side to this principle of reward, that forms a background to, and will exert a strong influence on, our final reward. This is the matter of motive, the great well-spring from which our service flows. The Lord gives us guidance in Matthew 6. Those who serve with men in view have no reward from their Father in heaven; the reward is here and now in the plaudits of men - "They have received their reward".

As we seek to serve the Lord according to the gift given to us and the gracious help of the Holy Spirit, we should have before us 1 Thessalonians 1:3 - "your work of faith and labour of love and patience of hope in our Lord Jesus Christ, before our God and Father". In faith, love and hope we have a foundation on which to build our lives of service for the Lord.

Faith

"Without faith it is impossible to be well pleasing unto Him, for he that cometh to God must believe that He is, and that He is a rewarder of them that seek after Him" (Hebrews 11:6). We serve, having before us Ecclesiastes 11:6: "In the morning sow thy seed, and in the evening withold not thine hand: for thou knowest not which shall prosper, whether this or that, or whether they both shall be alike good".

Love

We love because He first loved us. As we consider love, Calvary looms in our view and what the Saviour did for us. Our service flows out from hearts that seek to return that love again. Calvary moulds our attitudes and our service.

Hope

"Be patient therefore, brethren, until the coming of the Lord. Behold, the husbandman waiteth for the precious fruit of the earth, being patient over it, until it receive the early and latter rain. Be ye also patient; stablish your hearts: for the coming of the Lord is at hand" (James 5:7,8).

We have come across these expressions elsewhere. "But now abideth faith, hope, love, these three; and the greater of these is love" (1 Corinthians 13:13 RV margin). Faith and hope are great but greater love will lead to a greater giving in service and to a greatness of reward, as was the experience of the woman in Luke 7:36-50. If faith, love, hope coupled with patience, give rise to our service it may be that when the day of review comes we shall hear from our Master the lovely words of appreciation and reward, "Well done, good and faithful servant (bondservant-slave): thou hast been faithful over a few things, I will set thee over many things: enter thou into the joy of thy Lord" (Mat. 25:21). May we hear and respond to the word, "Go ye also into the vineyard, and whatsoever is right I will give you".

CHAPTER EIGHT: SELF-ASSURANCE AND FAILURE

Caesarea Philippi became a high-water mark in Peter's experience. Then, with joy and confidence, he declared, "Thou art the Christ, the Son of the living God". Months later, in the courtyard of the High Priest in Jerusalem, a different Peter emerged. Now, at a low point of his disciple life, with oaths and curses he says of his Master, "I know not the man". What brought about this change?

With obvious leadership qualities, Peter's natural instinct would be to master any situation by his own strength. Though sincere, warmhearted and responsive, under extreme pressure he became vulnerable through his self-assertiveness. His home life lay within the influence of a close-knit fishing community of family and friends. As one of the Twelve, he knew the warmth of loving companionship and fellowship with the Master and others. Peter's story is a warning to us, as we see him in ourselves. Matthew 26:30-75 introduces us to three highly charged incidents. How did Peter respond?

The Mount of Olives (vv. 30-35)

The Lord had clearly warned of the Devil's snare. God was about to smite His Shepherd, resulting in the scattering abroad of the flock. Peter impulsively contradicts such predictions. The severe rebuke of Peter in Matthew 16:23, "Get thee behind Me, Satan", had for the time being been forgotten. Luke provides additional insight into the Lord's foreknowledge and forewarnings, and also His prayer on Peter's behalf (22:31,32).

Satan desired to have the Twelve that he might sift them as wheat The Lord made request to His Father that Peter's faith would not fail. The emphatic repudiation by Peter of even the possibility of such faithlessness, was thoroughly characteristic of his affections, yet also of his self-confidence (Luke 22:33; Matthew 26:33).

Here, as he claimed exemption from self-weakness, he admitted that others might fall away! Peter was too self-assured. As the snare was closing because of his own undetected weaknesses and Satan's wiles, he said, "I will not deny Thee". The Lord, in predicting Peter's almost immediate downfall, would no doubt do so with great sorrow. What Peter had said, likewise said also all the disciples. The fault lay not so much in the willing declaration of their love as in misunderstanding the divine purpose in the crucifixion. With the Lord's help and guidance, let us learn from Peter's experience to heed the Lord's timely warnings and be aware of human weakness.

Gethsemane (vv. 36-56)

Our present study is not to comment on the Lord's intense agony and sorrow in the Garden, but rather to observe the actions of Peter. To him the Lord said, "What, could ye not watch with Me one hour? Watch and pray, that ye enter not into temptation: the spirit indeed is willing, but the flesh is weak" (Matthew 26:40,41). The Lord again warned of the trials that lay ahead for Peter. As Judas, accompanied by the great multitude came with their swords to arrest Jesus, Peter having a sword (John 18:10), drew it in an impulsive attack, striking off the right ear of Malchus, servant to the High Priest. Jesus, on healing Malchus (Luke 22:51), turned to Peter and said, "Put up the sword into the sheath: the cup which the Father hath given Me, shall I not drink it?" (John 18:11).

Peter's display of zeal may well have been but a conspicuous show of mingled affection and self-confidence. The Lord's past discourses and admonitions made such a militant response look absurd. Peter disregarded the risks to himself and to the other disciples, yet behind all these events, the Lord knew of a better day for Peter "When once thou has turned again, stablish thy brethren" (Luke 22:32).

Let us guard against impulsive actions. One act of mistaken zeal done in the strength of the flesh can lead to circumstances fraught with dire consequences. Like Peter, we can so easily be caught off guard as ready prey for the Adversary. Our need too, is to watch and pray against temptation.

In the Courtyard (vv. 57-75)

"They that had taken Jesus led Him away to ... Caiaphas the High Priest ... Peter followed Him afar off, into the court ... and sat with the officers, to see the end". Sad reading indeed! Peter's actions show bewilderment as events so rapidly unfolded; events he obviously was not ready to accept. Had recent occurrences disillusioned him as they did others, who said, "We hoped that it was He which should redeem Israel" (Luke 24:21)? It was not the time for the kingdom to be restored (Acts 1:6). No doubt Peter had with great excitement and anticipation entered Jerusalem with his Messiah. He had heard Him acclaimed by the multitude: "Hosanna to the Son of David". Now that vision was dimmed, almost extinguished.

The Upper Room experiences, the feet washing, the Passover supper, the startling words of the Lord as He announced His imminent death, His pronouncement of a New Covenant, the betrayal by Judas, the Malchus incident, the admonitions by his Master, all were bringing great pressure and confusion to Peter's mind and hearing His faith was being tried; the wheat sifting process by the Adversary was well under way. His morale so low, disturbed, disappointed, dejected, Peter followed afar off - "to see the end". Although there had been ample warnings by the Lord against Peter's self-assurance, bravado and pride, still, "he spake exceeding vehemently, If I must die with Thee, I will not deny Thee. And in like manner also said they all" (Mark 14:31), all guilty with Peter of defection in this hour of crisis.

So, without heeding the Master's warnings, Peter denied the One he truly loved. Full of self-confidence and lapsing in loyalty, he chose to ignore the danger signals; his denials were emphatically reinforced before his tormentors, with oaths and curses. The old nature reasserted itself, perhaps to distract and play for time which was fast running out. It may be that we all have our breaking point, and Peter had reached his in an unexpected way saying, "I know not the Man". Group pressure had become too much for him to take. In his Master's hour of need, he had denied Him three times.

How dangerous then it is for us as Christians to sit as Peter did, in compromising company, and to warm ourselves by the enemy's fire. One denial leads to another and another. Peter failed as a friend and companion. It is when we are up against it that we need loyal, courageous and trusting friends, yet the Lord knew that all would forsake Him and flee. Thankfully, in Him we have a friend that sticks closer than a brother. "And straightway the cock crew". The pathos and drama of Peter's night was almost over, but for the Lord so much more lay ahead. Peter suddenly remembered what the Lord had said, and he went out weeping bitter tears of sincere repentance.

The Look of Love (Luke 22:61)

"And the Lord turned and looked upon Peter ... and Peter remembered". Only Luke tells of this poignant moment, enacted perhaps as Jesus was being led away to Pilate. It brought home to Peter not only the nature of his guilt, but also the arresting love of his Master, saving him from total despair and ruin. "Wherefore let him that thinketh he standeth take heed lest he fall" (1 Corinthians 10:12).

By the Sea (John 21:7, 15-22)

Three denials brought three requests from the Lord for love to be demonstrated. The wounds of Peter's denials were so fresh, so deep, that the hurt was still there. Could he any longer be trusted? Could he trust even his own emotions, commitment and love to his Lord and to others? The Lord who warned of denial, foretold also the turning again, and the stablishing of Peter's brethren through his restoration. "Lovest thou Me more than these?" (Greek: Agapao, a real affection for, exercised in an active and devoted way). "Yea, Lord; Thou knowest that I love Thee" (Greek: Phileo, a fondness and natural affection for). What will our response be? The Lord longs for real love from devoted hearts, just as He sought this from Peter.

The Lord would yet be honoured by a changed Peter, one preserved by Him to love and serve in deed and truth. It was indeed a reflective Peter who later, against the background of personal experience, wrote to other saints facing trials: "That the proof of your faith ... though it is proved by fife, might be found unto praise" (1 Peter 1:7). And again, "If ye are reproached for the Name of Christ, blessed are ye ... if a man suffer as a Christian, let him not be ashamed" (1 Peter 4:1-16).

What a warning Peter's early life story is to us. Should we fall, or fail our Lord, he longs to grant us restoration to Himself through repentance. "He Himself hath suffered being tempted, He is able to succour them that are tempted" (Hebrews 2:18). The roughest diamond can be cut and polished by the divine

Lapidary if we allow ourselves to be so transformed by Him. "To Him who is able to keep you from falling ... be glory, majesty, power and authority" (Jude 24 NIV).

CHAPTER NINE: HE RESTORES MY SOUL

There are some bright and attractive steam locomotives near my home. In fine working order, they bring pleasure to many; yet they are almost unrecognizable from the dull, unworkable things they once were. The great change occurred through the patient work of the restorer. At Calvary, the great restorer of souls demonstrated His infinite love for both His Father and ourselves when He fulfilled His commitment made in eternity and revealed in Messianic Psalm, "Though I have stolen nothing, I still must restore it" (Psalm 69:4). And that love, patience and commitment to restoration are undiminished today, as He transforms the life of many a failing Christian. We see this so vividly illustrated in His gracious restoration of the apostle Peter.

Having considered his sad failure in the previous chapter, we now trace the process of his complete restoration. And we do so mindful of the fact that though we are not called to such prominent service as Peter's, we are called to serve the same gracious Lord. Conscious of failure ourselves, we find his experience a great encouragement. The Lord Himself lovingly takes the initiative in such restoration, clearly demonstrated by three aspects of His restoring of Peter.

Firstly, He prayed for it: "I have prayed for you, that your faith should not fail" (Luke 22:32). It is a great comfort to struggling Christians today to know that this same compassionate Friend "ever lives to make intercession for them" (Hebrews 7:25). And those who would be much used by their Lord will, like Peter, he prime targets of Satan. They will need the prayers of others too.

Secondly, He promised it: "When thou art converted, strengthen thy brethren" (Luke 22:32 KJV). This does not mean that restoration is ever automatic; it is only as God graciously grants repentance (2 Timothy 2:25). However, it is fitting that Peter himself tells us "the Lord ... is longsuffering toward us ... that all should come to repentance" (2 Peter 3:9).

Thirdly, He prompted it: "The Lord turned (Greek: strepho) and looked at Peter" (Luke 22:61), and this started the process by which he became converted (Greek: epistrepho - turned about). Yes, "'Tis the look that melted Peter", filling his eyes with tears and his heart with sorrow. But thankfully, then as now, "godly sorrow produces repentance" (2 Corinthians 7:10).

We try to imagine poor Peter's awful state that weekend. Broken-hearted that his dearest Friend, the Messiah, had been brutally slain, he also carried a heavy burden of guilt; he had let his Lord down so badly, even to the extent of lying and cursing in the process. No wonder he wept bitterly! "I'm not worthy of Him, I'm finished" he might have thought. But "Peter remembered the word of the Lord" (Luke 22:61) who so accurately predicted his failure, and on reflection this surely gave him hope; for it reinforced the fact that the Lord had chosen him even though He knew the worst about him! Perhaps too, in his grief he clung to the Lord's promise regarding his conversion. So today in our darkest hours of failure and self-doubt, when Satan would smash our faith, we can cling to the rock of Christ's promises until the storm has passed.

On the glorious resurrection morning restoring grace was already working in Peter, for although he had wept bitterly he had not remained isolated, wallowing in destructive self-pity. He was in fact with John, and characteristically he was the first apostle to enter tile empty tomb, eager to know the truth. The stupendous news of Christ's resurrection would have been greeted with mixed feelings by Peter. "How shall I meet those eyes?" would sum up how he felt, no doubt. However, there was real encouragement for him in the heavenly message to the women that his Lord was thinking specially of him, for the angel said, "Go and tell his disciples - and Peter - that He is going before you into Galilee; there you will see Him" (Mark 16:7). And indeed among the apostles the risen Lord gave priority to Peter: "He appeared to Cephas (Peter); then to the twelve" (1 Corinthians 15:5 RV). This is confirmed by the message of the disciples late on the resurrection day, "The Lord is risen indeed, and has appeared to Simon!" (Luke 24:34).

Yes, the Lord was going to demonstrate His tremendous grace by restoring the one who had publicly failed Him, and transform him into an outstanding and courageous leader of His people. So an early face-to-face alone with Peter was essential. We are not told what was said at that crucial interview, but we may be sure it was heart-to-heart, when true repentance and complete and loving forgiveness were fully expressed. Some time later, the first apostle into the empty tomb was first into the water to meet the Lord on the beach that morning after the fruitless fishing trip. Peter's eagerness to be near his risen Lord was a sure sign that communion had been restored.

Having lovingly assured Peter of his forgiveness, the Lord was ready to confront him with the renewed challenge of true discipleship. Three years earlier Peter had been irresistibly drawn by the Man who said, "Follow Me", and after all that had happened since, the last recorded words of the risen Christ to Peter personally, spoken that morning by the lake, were still, "Follow Me" (John 21:19). From first to last, and at every stage, the Christian's life should be a personal response to Christ, with a genuine desire to follow His teaching, His example, and indeed the Man Himself in personal devotion and communion. Any so-called "advancement" in Christian service which takes one away from such devotion to the Lord is not true progress. This was a vital lesson for Peter who was to shoulder the responsibility of leadership among God's New Covenant people. And it is a crucial lesson for any who would be leaders among God's people today.

But before Peter's brethren could be expected to accept such leadership from one who had seriously failed by a three-fold denial of his Lord, Peter needed to face both the challenge and the opportunity of demonstrating his genuine restoration by a corresponding three-fold declaration of his love for the Lord in the presence of such brethren. And furthermore, like us today, Peter needed to know what "Follow Me" means in practice. These issues were faced that morning by the lake, and the earnest conversation is recorded for us in John 21. We understand that the writer used two different Greek words, both translated love, to convey just what was said. In seeking to understand the conversation better, an amplification along the following lines might be of some help.

> JESUS: Simon ... do you truly love Me with all your being, more than these do?
>
> PETER: Yes Lord, You know that I have a loving affection for You.
>
> JESUS: Feed My lambs.
>
> (Again, the same question received the same answer, then:)
>
> JESUS: Tend My sheep. (And finally:) Simon, do you really and truly have such a loving affection for Me?

(Peter, who now mistrusted his old self-confidence, didn't feel worthy to claim the higher agape love of his entire being, but when Jesus challenged even his affection for him, this hurt. He was sure his Lord knew his love, and just how strong or weak it would prove to be).

PETER: Lord, You know all things. You know I have this loving affection for You.

JESUS: Feed My sheep.

Like Peter, we do not feel we can boast of our love either; nevertheless, we do love our Lord and we want to follow Him more closely. And as the Lord impressed upon Peter that day, such following in loving response to Christ entails caring about others. This is a challenge to us all, especially to those who, like Peter, are called to be shepherds among the Lord's people. True commitment means tender caring.

Peter and the other apostles continued learning from the Lord until His ascension. Then in both waiting for and witnessing by the Holy Spirit, Peter's restoration to spiritual leadership was clearly demonstrated. For, less than two months earlier in a Jerusalem courtyard, "Simon Peter stood up and warmed himself" (John 18:25), yet failed hopelessly to stand up for his Master. But during the ten days' wait for the Holy Spirit, "Peter stood up in the midst of the disciples" (Acts 1:15) and led the one hundred and twenty in seeking a successor to Judas. Then at Pentecost, filled with the Holy Spirit and facing thousands, "Peter standing up ... raised his voice and said ..." (Acts 2:14), and we know the marvellous result - thousands were saved when restored Peter began to take his stand for Christ.

In future chapters, we shall trace his faithful, fruitful, and fearless progress; a glorious testimony to the restorer of souls who lovingly renewed the invitation, "Follow Me". Meantime, we conclude our present study marvelling at the restoring grace which made Peter a more effective disciple than ever he had been before. Such recovery to fruitful service, which is to the glory of God and the blessing of others was, we recall, in the heart of repentant David when he pleaded, "Restore to me the joy of Your salvation ... then I will teach transgressors Your ways, and sinners shall be converted to You" (Psalm 51:12,13). The vital sequence implied in this psalm is repentance, restoration, revival, and results. We have seen this so clearly in Peter's experience.

So those of us who are conscious of failure and deeply desire to be restored to a Spirit-filled life, well-pleasing to the Lord, are encouraged by God's gracious promise: "I will restore to you the years that the swarming locust has eaten" (Joel 2:25). May it be so in many lives to His glory.

"Wilt Thou restore?

Then Lord in faith

Before Thy feet I bow,

Confess to Thee my shame and loss.

Fulfil Thy promise now,

Thus changed and sanctified, made meet

To do the humblest task;

To be well pleasing in Thy sight

My Lord, is all I ask."

CHAPTER TEN: DO YOU LOVE ME?

Waiting times can often be testing times, and many great men have broken down in the test of frustration and inactivity which such times can bring. Intentionally or unintentionally they have repudiated solemn commitments and have deranged true priorities. In spiritual experience, it is wise to wait on the Lord and to wait for the Lord; to wait for the assurance of the divine will and purpose, and to wait for the divine leading as to response. Such waiting times should not be frustrating.

After His resurrection, the Lord Jesus intermittently visited His disciples, strengthening their faith and instructing them in His will for them. The intervals between His visits were obviously testing times. During these intervals, Christ was physically absent from His disciples and doubtless this brought to them a feeling of emptiness. They missed their Saviour and Lord. He was so loving, so gracious, so gentle and so authoritative that when He withdrew from the disciples the void seemed unbearable. Empty indeed is the life from which Christ is absent.

It was in one of these breaks that Simon Peter exclaimed, "I'm going fishing". Perhaps he had heard the lapping of the waves. This would be music to his ears. He may have gazed wistfully at the boats setting off for the fishing grounds. Here was activity that attracted him. The pull of the sea was strong. For a vigorous person like Peter inactivity meant boredom. He could bear it no longer. "I'm going fishing". There was nothing wrong with the respectable, honourable and beneficial occupation of fishing, but one day Peter had heard a voice which said, "Fear not; from henceforth thou shalt catch men". The Speaker was the Lord, the Christ, and Peter's heart had been won. He left all and followed

Him. When, therefore, he said, "I'm going fishing" had his vision become blurred, had the impression of his commitment been erased, had his priorities been disturbed?

Peter was a leader, and as a forceful man he had the ability to influence others. The effect of his declaration of intent was immediate. The six other disciples said, "We also come with thee". Without suggesting that Peter had in his mind any purpose of drawing the other disciples away from what was right we may, perhaps, in this meditation draw attention to two things which impress us:

(1) Persons who have influence on others should be responsibly concerned as to what they influence other people to do. This is a most serious matter for consideration.

(2) On the other hand, we need to be careful about those under whose influence we place ourselves. There are persons with strong minds and strong wills, but who are themselves subject to the Lord's authority. Under their influence we may find the direction in life and may receive encouragement to spiritual purpose and determination. Others of similar natural character may be guilty of spiritual licence and lawlessness. Under their influence disciples of the Lord may be misled to accept and to engage in things which are contrary to God's will. Such persons may be blatant or they may be suave. We need to be on our guard. Paul said, "Be not deceived: Evil company doth corrupt good manners" (1 Corinthians 15:33). Many senior disciples have deeply regretted that in their early years they placed themselves in the dangers of wrong influence.

As dawn broke over Tiberias, seven disappointed and crestfallen men made for the shore. How miserable these physically and spiritually hungry men must have felt! Their Lord and Master was missing. And they had no fish. Perhaps they reflected on the occasions when the lovely Man had been with them in the boat. Memory is a remarkable faculty and memories may be sweet, but they can be painful. They may also deepen our longings for those whose companionship and fellowship we have lost. We are trying to think of the state of mind in which the disciples may have been as they neared the beach.

In the light of early morning they saw a lone Figure standing on the land, but they did not recognize Him. The Stranger spoke first. "Children, have ye aught to eat?" Concern, sympathy and love were revealed in this question. "Cast the net on the right side of the boat". These were words of authority and command. Why without question the disciples responded may be difficult to explain, but at least those disconsolate men seemed to feel an irresistible influence in the command of the Stranger. The Lord whom they had lost was back with them to work in their hearts. A great work of grace was taking place. As the fishermen towed the fish-crammed net John looked again at the Stranger. "It is the Lord", he said to Peter. He might have used other titles to identify the Man on the beach, but do not let us miss the significance of the one he did use. "It is the Lord" - the One who called us, the One who owns us, the One to whom we are committed, the One for whose sake we left all that we might follow Him and serve Him in loving obedience. Their blessed Lord was coming right back into the centre of their lives, and with what amazing grace did He do so!

One feels persuaded that He came to the very place from which they had set out on their abortive fishing expedition. But there was no rebuke. On the beach the disciples saw a kindled fire, bread and fish. What a welcome! What affectionate understanding! "Come and break your fast", said the gracious Lord. Here was communion of a very practical kind, and here was assurance that the disciples were in the presence of One who not only loved them but who also knew their needs, and was fully able to supply them.

Many disciples of Christ have at times felt that they have lost their Lord. Things of time and earth, perhaps things which in themselves are quite legitimate, move in to fill our lives. We obey the dictates of worldly interests. Friendships, the demands of employment, the cares of this life, earthly pleasures, personal ambitions - any or all of these we may attempt to substitute for the Lord. Then the vanity of these things depresses us. Our very unhappiness is but proof of what in happier days we sang with sincere appreciation, "Now none but Christ can satisfy". From stricken hearts we may have cried with Mary Magdalene, "They have taken away my Lord, and I know not where they have laid Him". But there He is ready to reveal Himself, waiting to draw us back to Himself, desirous of restoring fellowship which brings Him into the centre of our lives. How gracious He is! How forgiving!

After the men had broken their fast there came for Simon Peter the searching climax of that remarkable day. Perhaps in the minds of the disciples there was the query, What are we going to do now? On a later occasion they asked the Lord, "Dost Thou at this time restore the kingdom to Israel?" But there were other great matters which the disciples had to learn and some of these things emerge from Peter's experience. Turning to him the Lord said, "Simon, son of John, lovest thou Me more than these?" Profound must have been the impact of this question on the rugged Peter and on each of the disciples present. Just prior to the crucifixion of Christ Peter had averred, "Although all shall be offended (caused to stumble) yet will not I" (Mark 14:29). Three times the searching question enters the heart of Peter. Three times he gives an affirmative answer. The deep inner searching which he was experiencing revealed itself in the words wrung from the heart of Simon Peter, "Lord, Thou knowest all things, Thou knowest that I love Thee".

It has been pointed out that the word for 'love' which the Lord used in the first and second questions was different from the word which Peter used in each of his three replies. In the third question the Lord adopted Peter's word. Of the significance of these two words one has said: "The first (agapao) expresses a more reasoning attachment, of choice and selection ... from a seeing in the object upon whom it is bestowed that which is worthy of regard; or else from a sense that such is due toward the person so regarded, as a benefactor, or the like; while the second (phileo), without being necessarily an unreasoning attachment, does yet give less account of itself to itself; is more instinctive, is more of the feelings or natural affections, implies more passion" (Dr. R. C. Trench). Three times Peter used the second word.

Responsibility in divine service is based on personal love for Christ. A man may have acute and profound knowledge. He may possess a burning zeal for activity. But if love for Christ is lacking all this profits nothing. On his acknowledgment of love for Christ Peter was commissioned for very important service. Would we serve the Lord? Would we work for Him? These are healthy desires. But perhaps we need the experience of the Tiberias beach. Have we in the Lord's presence heard from Him the enquiry, Do you love me? Never mind what the Lord has in His purpose for other disciples. Here is something for me.

Can I say "You know all things; You know that I love You. I love You because of who You are, because of the greatness of Your Being and the perfection of Your attributes, because of the wondrous things which in unspeakable grace You have done for me. And as I have by that same grace come to know something of the beauty and sweetness of Your character, Your loveliness in its many manifestations, I find my heart stirred and moved by warm affection. You know."

CHAPTER ELEVEN: PETER AND THE MEEKNESS AND GENTLENESS OF CHRIST

I have been interested recently in the expression in 2 Corinthians 10:1, 'the meekness and gentleness of Christ'. In an essay of that name, James Martin defined meekness as 'love suffering' and gentleness as 'love serving'; meekness as 'love in repose', gentleness as 'love in action'; meekness as 'love bearing evil', gentleness as 'love doing good'. I've looked at the meekness and gentleness of Christ in some of the closing scenes of His life in which Peter also features prominently. It's not intended as a character assassination of Peter, but to show up these characteristics of his Lord.

Meekness

Many Bible students suggest that the words 'meek' and 'meekness' indicate not just a person's outward behaviour, but 'an inward grace of the soul', the exercises of which are first and foremost towards God. 'It is that temper of spirit in which we accept His dealings with us as good, and therefore without disputing or resisting'. Being primarily an acceptance of God's dealings, it also manifests itself to others especially in the face of insult or injury, recognising that such hurt may be allowed or employed by God for His glory. It is difficult to translate into English, for our terms meekness and mildness usually seem to have a connotation of weakness. The Greek word definitely has no such thought. It was demonstrated by the Lord Himself and commended to His followers as the fruit of inner strength. A person is not, as is commonly suggested, meek because he cannot help himself. The Lord was meek, yet had the infinite resources of God at His command. Meekness is the result of controlled strength and is the opposite of self-assertiveness and self-interest.

Gentleness

Vine says that gentleness denotes fairness, moderation, sweet reasonableness. Of the adjective, Trench says that it denotes, 'seemly, fitting; hence equitable, fair, moderate, forbearing, not insisting on the letter of the law'. A gentle person knows when to apply the law and when not to apply it. His first concern is not to stand for his legal rights, but to bring Christian love to bear on a situation.

Peter seems to fail frequently in those closing days of His Lord's earthly ministry: twice in the upper room, when he missed the opportunity to wash his Lord's feet and then protested that the Lord would never wash his feet; in the garden when, three times, he was supposed to be at prayer and when he drew the sword; and three times when he denied his Lord in the high priest's court. Other disciples failed in some of those respects; Peter in all of them, but he served a Man who was both meek and gentle.

In the Upper Room

Peter, who, with John had seen the unusual sight of a man bearing a pitcher of water, and had followed him to the house, failed to see his opportunity to wash the Lord's feet. Meekly, without remonstrating, the Lord set aside his garments in a little cameo of His greater stoop from heaven's glory, and began gently to wash their feet. The meekness and gentleness of Christ was expressed by love in repose, then love in action.

A sudden silence must have fallen over the group, as the Lord passed from one to another in this lowly ministry. Then, Peter, ashamed and indignant, made his second mistake. He protested mildly. "Lord, are You washing my feet?" (John 13:6) and then added more vehemently, "You shall never wash my feet!" (v.8) It's a strong word, 'never': the absolute negative. The Lord, who had listened with such uncomplaining meekness to their quarrelsome aspirations of greatness, stooped then in gentleness and explained to Peter the distinct necessities of bathing for 'union' and washing for 'communion'. How meekly and gently the Lord turned around Peter's strong assertion that the Lord would never wash his feet. What He'd taught them in word earlier when He'd said, 'Take My yoke upon you ... for I am meek' (Matthew 11:29 Revised Version), He now showed them in deed.

Up Olivet

We move now to Olivet, the scene of Peter's next mistakes, to witness again the meekness and gentleness of Christ. Three disciples, including Peter, are taken deeper into the shadows of the olive trees and asked to watch and pray. Returning to them, the Lord found them sleeping, and, addressing Peter, He asked, "Simon (the name suggestive of his weakness), are you sleeping?" Disappointed, and alone, He went back to His lonely spot a stone's throw away and, in an agony of blood-like sweat, He poured out His plea a second time. Finding them asleep a third time, how was He now going to respond? The hireling would have fled, but the Good Shepherd stands over them watchfully, "Sleep on now, and take your rest" (Mark 14:41 RV). What a choice time, in His hour of agony and loneliness, to fulfil His promise of Matthew 11:28, "Come to Me, all you who labour and are heavy laden, and I will give you rest" (same word). How meek and gentle of Him to oversee their own refreshment as the motley mob headed by Judas approached the garden to seize Him!

The apostles all misread the situation, and Peter in particular. He was no coward. He would fight like a lion, if the Lord permitted it. "Put your sword in its place, for all who take the sword will perish by the sword." In that quiet, yet authoritative manner, the Lord ensured that there would be no unseemly struggle which Peter's impulsive act might otherwise have prompted.

In the High Priest's Court

The band, their Captive in their midst, headed back to the city. John gained entry into the palace of Annas, but, not discovering Peter, and sure that he was waiting outside, went back and spoke on his friend's behalf to the maid. She admitted Peter who joined the group at the fire and stood and warmed himself. There followed the denial to the fortress, to another maid and to those who said that his speech gave him away. While he was denying his Lord the third time, the cock crowed a second time and the Lord turned and looked at Peter. The word means he could see him clearly. Not a long stare, that's a different word. But the look broke Peter. Why? Perhaps because Peter remembered that look. It was the same way in which He first looked at him. John (1:42) uses the same word of that first encounter. Andrew 'brought him to Jesus. Now when Jesus looked at him, He said, "You are Simon the son of Jonah. You shall be called Cephas" (which is translated, A Stone)'. Peter had let his Lord down; he'd been anything but a stone, more the old quicksand Simon.

That's where the writers leave him. A penitent man weeping bitterly, wailing out aloud. Does his Lord leave him there? Not at all. 'For a righteous man may fall seven times and rise again' (Proverbs 24:16). No-one else mentions it, but Mark, in whose writings scholars say they can see the unmistakable influence of Peter, in recounting the early morning visit of the women to the tomb, recalls that the young man sitting in the tomb said to them, "Go, tell His disciples - and Peter." Peter had failed Him in the garden and in the judgement hall, but still the Lord remembered him tenderly and sent him an individual message. The meekness and gentleness of Christ! Then, with added grace, we read in 1 Corinthians 15:3-5 that "Christ ... was seen by Cephas." That private meeting is confirmed in Luke 24:34: "The Lord is risen indeed, and has appeared to Simon!" How gracious! How wonderfully meek and gentle!

On the Beach

We come finally to the night's fishing and the breakfast on the beach. The most striking thing about that breakfast is the change in Peter. We recall again the proverb that a righteous man may fall seven times and rise again. How grateful Peter would be that the Lord had lovingly extended the limits of forgiveness from Peter's seven times to the Lord's seventy times seven! The Lord's meekness and gentleness during the experience of the past days had taught him some important lessons. He had learned his own weakness. There was no boastful statement about his love or his courage, or about being better than anyone else. He didn't even use the same word for 'love' in his answer as Jesus used in His question. Jesus asked, "Do you love (agapao) Me?" meaning devoted, self-giving love. Peter answered, "I love (phileo) You", meaning, 'Yes, I love You as a friend.'

David says in Psalm 18, "Your gentleness has made me great". We can follow Peter's life now through the early chapters of the Acts as he's at the helm of the work, firstly, dramatically, with the Jews, and then gradually, gently, among the Gentiles in Acts 10. How had the change come about? Surely, with true humility, Peter would say the same thing as David, the Lord's "gentleness has made me great".

CHAPTER TWELVE: THE POWER OF HIS RESURRECTION

Our title is taken from Philippians 3:10 where the apostle Paul speaks of his desire to know by experience the power of Christ's resurrection in his own life. The power he desired was that same power he referred to in Ephesians 1:19,20 when he spoke of knowing, "what is the exceeding greatness of His power toward us who believe, according to the working of His mighty power which He worked in Christ when He raised Him from the dead and seated Him at His right hand in the heavenly places". The Greek word for power in the original is 'dunamis', meaning miraculous power, ability, strength, power. We might call such power God's dynamite! This power God exerted in raising Christ from the dead, and it was the power Paul desired in his life and the power Peter now demonstrated in his preaching, firstly as recorded in Acts 2 on the Day of Pentecost and then in Acts 3 when, after healing of the lame man, he challenged his Jewish hearers to repent and be converted (Acts 3:19).

Peter's Power

How was it that Peter, having denied his Master three times with oaths and curses, should now be found witnessing for his Lord, preaching the gospel with power and authority? The answer is that he was a changed man for, on the Day of Pentecost, along with the other disciples, he received the blessing of the outpouring and indwelling of the Holy Spirit. This was a direct fulfilment of God's promise to them as foretold by the Lord Jesus. He had said, "But you shall receive power when the Holy Spirit has come upon you; and you shall be witnesses to Me in Jerusalem, and in all Judea and Samaria, and to the end of the earth" (Acts 1:8).

That power, dunamis, was now Peter's and the other disciples' as a result of the outpouring and indwelling of the Holy Spirit. Standing up with the eleven, Peter preached a powerful message to those at Jerusalem, showing they must bear direct responsibility for rejecting and then crucifying their Messiah. His message is clear and succinct. "Men of Israel, hear these words: Jesus of Nazareth, a Man attested by God to you by miracles, wonders, and signs which God did through Him in your midst, as you yourselves also know - Him, being delivered by the carefully planned intention and foreknowledge of God, you have taken by lawless hands, have crucified, and put to death" (Acts 2:22,23).

Peter's Message

In tracing through Peter's discourse, it is evident that all he has to say is summarized in Acts 2:36, "Therefore let all the house of Israel know assuredly that God has made this Jesus, whom you crucified, both Lord and Christ", and in challenging his hearers with the reality of the power of Christ's resurrection he deals with three vital truths related to the outpouring of the Holy Spirit:

1. It was a fulfilment of prophecy - vv.16-21.

2. Jesus Christ was their Messiah and the One they rejected - vv.22-32.

3. Through the finished work of Jesus Christ, the glorified Messiah, God has now poured out the Holy Spirit - vv.33-36.

Thus, having shown that this was all in God's will, Peter challenges their hearts as to how they must respond - vv.37-39.

Joel's Prophecy

The prophecy is taken from Joel, and Pentecost was a partial fulfilment of the prophecy, for as verse 20 shows, some of what Joel spoke about will not be fulfilled, "before the coming of the great and notable day of the LORD". A day of future judgement for the nations of this world, after which, the Lord Jesus establishes His thousand-year kingdom on earth. See also 1 Thessalonians 5:2; 2 Thessalonians 1:10; 2:2; 2 Peter 3:10. Under the guidance of the Holy Spirit Peter shows that the events of Pentecost were not the acts of drunken men, but the powerful manifestation of the promised Holy Spirit now given to believers to indwell them as a sign of their salvation. Then as now it is true that, "whoever calls on the Name of the Lord shall be saved" (Acts 2:21).

The Thrust of the Message

What was special in the preaching of the message on that day was that those to whom Peter spoke were the ones who had rejected their Messiah. For them it was necessary they should clearly understand the seriousness of what they had done. So he says, "Him, being delivered by the carefully planned intention and foreknowledge of God, you have taken by lawless hands, have crucified, and put to death" (Acts 2:23). Two things are emphasized:

    1. The crucifixion was no accident, but was in God's set purpose.

2. Peter's listeners, nevertheless, were directly responsible for Christ's death and accountable to God for their actions.

Further, in verse 24, Peter clearly shows it was the exertion of God's power which had raised Christ from the dead, "having loosed the pains of death, because it was not possible that He should be held by it", concluding, "Therefore let all the house of Israel know assuredly that God has made this Jesus, whom you crucified, both Lord and Christ" (verse 36). This is the reality of the power of Christ's resurrection.

What Shall We Do?

So powerful was Peter's message, and so evident the working of the Holy Spirit, that those who heard were "... cut to the heart" and said, "Men and brethren, what shall we do?" (Acts 2:37). They were under conviction of sin, having now been brought to the point where they could receive through faith in Christ, the forgiveness of sins and the gift of the indwelling Holy Spirit. This was only the beginning, for there needed to be the practical outworking of their faith in obedience to the Lord's teaching as to serving Him in the Church of God in Jerusalem.

So we read, "Then those who gladly received His word were baptized; and that day about three thousand souls were added to them. And they continued steadfastly in the apostles' doctrine and fellowship, in the breaking of bread, and in prayers" (Acts 2:41,42). It has been well pointed out that the first three steps, belief in the gospel, baptism and addition to the Church of God in Jerusalem were things which would not need to be repeated while the final four, continuance in the truths of the doctrine, fellowship, breaking of the bread and the assembly prayers would need steadfastness on the part of those who had been added. These were days of powerful testimony and blessing. Those who responded to the challenge, "continuing daily with one accord in the temple ... praising God and having favour with all the people. And the Lord added to the church daily those who were being saved" (Acts 2:46,47).

A Lame Man Healed

The healing of the lame man in Acts 3 provided further opportunity for the preaching of the gospel in all its power and fullness, and for testimony to be given to the power of Christ's resurrection. The incident concerned a man who was over forty years old and, having been lame all his life, was carried every day to one of the temple gates, where he would beg for money. As Peter and John had approached him Peter, looking directly at him, had caused the man to think he was about to give him money, whereas, speaking in the Name of the Lord Peter proclaimed: "Silver and gold I do not have, but what I do have I give you: In the Name of Jesus Christ of Nazareth, rise up and walk" (Acts 3:6). Jesus of Nazareth, the King of the Jews was the title, John tells us, Pilate had placed over the Lord's Cross and to which the Jewish leaders had greatly objected (John 19:19-22). This was the Name and authority by which this miracle was now performed in the Temple precincts!

Repent Therefore and Be Converted

As Peter spoke to the crowd that then gathered to see the man who had been so wonderfully healed, he preached in the Name of the One they had rejected. "But you denied the Holy One and the Just, and asked for a murderer to be granted to you, and killed the Prince of life, whom God raised from the dead, of which we are witnesses" (Acts 3:14,15). The man had been healed through faith in Christ's Name. It was not sufficient that they should recognize they had killed the Prince of life, they must also be brought to the point of repentance and conversion. So he challenges, "Repent therefore and be converted, that your sins may be blotted out, so that times of refreshing may come from the presence of the Lord" (Acts 3:19), concluding, "To you first, God, having raised up His Servant Jesus, sent Him to bless you, in turning away every one of you from your iniquities" (Acts 3:26).

The ensuing chapters of Acts show how powerfully and clearly the message of the power of Christ's resurrection was preached and believed. Thousands were saved and added to the Church in Jerusalem. The truth of the power of Christ's resurrection is as vital today both in the preaching of the gospel, and in the daily experience of the disciple, as it was in the days of the apostles. The resurrection is central to Christian doctrine. The very next chapter of Acts records, "And with great power (dunamis) the apostles gave witness to the resurrection of the Lord Jesus. And great grace was upon them all" (Acts 4:33). That same power and grace should be seen in our lives today.

CHAPTER THIRTEEN: I AM READY

'Lord ... I am ready to go both to prison and to death', asserts Peter. No romantic idealism this, but words expressing his conviction that his Master is the Christ, the Son of the living God. Perhaps many times in the ensuing years he would recall his words, not we like to think, with any sense of regret for the sentiment expressed. True, there was much regret at his failure to give answer concerning the hope that was in him (1 Peter 3:15) when three times he denied the Lord, but the Master's prayer was answered. Faith did not fail, but was strengthened to allow him a ministry of strengthening his brethren. 'I am ready' would be tested many times.

At Tiberias, in resurrection, the Lord told Peter of the death by which he would glorify God (John 21:19; 2 Peter 1:14), and immediately said 'Follow Me'. Here is the cornerstone of true discipleship - following. 'Take up your cross and follow Me' was the Lord's clear directive, and for Peter this would mean a very real experience of the 'fellowship of His sufferings' (Philippians 3:10). Peter speaks of his decease in 2 Peter 1:14-15 and recalls the day when he was an eyewitness of the Lord's majesty when on that mountain He spoke of His decease, His great exodus from this world. It's not clear whether or not Peter heard His conversation with Moses and Elijah, but he would learn that before his Master could accomplish that decease He would have to endure all the suffering that was Calvary. 'I am ready'. Yes Peter, you too will have a path of suffering to tread before your decease.

Acts 4

'I am ready'. The will of God for disciples of this dispensation had been delivered to the apostles by their Lord (Acts 1), and following His ascension they exercised themselves in prayer, and after Pentecost, preaching. The Lord had come preaching the gospel of God, doing good and healing, and now the healing of this lame man and the subsequent preaching by Peter would bring into sharp focus for him the cost of following. "A servant is not greater than his lord. If they persecuted Me, they will also persecute you."

The fact of the change in the lame man could not be denied by the authorities (vv. 14-16), but they would not share in its joy. The means of achieving the miracle was to them a threat, just as the life of the Lord Jesus had been perceived as a threat to the stability of the nation, though it was for envy that He was delivered up (Matthew 27:18). He had forewarned His disciples that they too would have similar experiences – "they will deliver you up to councils ... but when they deliver you up be not anxious how or what ye shall speak ... it shall be given you in that hour what he shall speak" (Matthew 10:17,19).

How true these words were proved to be! Detained overnight because the authorities were sore troubled at the preaching of the apostles, they were brought before the intimidating presence of the council and cross-examined. 'Ignorant and unlearned men' perhaps, but "it is not you that speak but the Spirit of your Father that speaketh in you" (Matthew 10:21). And so, in the hour when their very faith was being tested, they displayed that spiritual boldness which is such a feature of Acts 4. Like a true deacon, Peter demonstrates "great boldness in the faith which is in Christ Jesus" (1 Timothy 3:13). Quite a change from earlier days!

When the disciple sincerely sanctifies in his heart Christ as Lord (1 Peter 3:15), when he totally commits himself to the Lord and His service, he will, like Peter, have to experience the fellowship of His sufferings in some measure. It may be, as Peter wrote, that the disciple's good manner of life in Christ will be reviled by some, but he says, it is better if God so wills, that you suffer for well-doing than for evil-doing (1 Peter 3:16,17). Whatever the test, to experience like Peter the reality of the Lord's promises at such a time is to gain great encouragement and a strengthening of faith.

And it was not only Peter and John who suffered. All the company of the disciples had fellowship with them in their experience. More than likely they had been praying for their release and when it came their reaction was to exercise themselves in further prayer: "grant unto Thy servants to speak Thy Word with all boldness". It was united prayer in the face of threatenings which touched heaven and brought an answer. "They were all filled with the Holy Spirit, and they spoke the Word of God with boldness" (v.31). God was working. Exercised prayer was answered! Threatenings, however, would lead to beatings, and with multiplied trials would come multiplied grace.

Acts 5

'I am ready'. The scene is set for confrontation. The Devil never gives up, and where God is working he is not very far away. Jerusalem is in a stir. The Church is growing: multitudes both of men and women. Many sick folk are healed. The Sadducees, who say there is no resurrection, neither angel nor spirit (Acts 23:8) imprison Peter and the apostles, but during the night they are released by an angel and told to continue to speak about this resurrection and spiritual life. They are re-arrested and charged 'you have filled Jerusalem with your teaching' - glorious fulfilment of the prayers of the disciples which we earlier considered. True, they had disobeyed the charge not to speak to all, nor teach in the Name of Jesus, but Peter's answer to this was uncompromising, 'we must obey God rather than men' (v.29).

This was not a deliberate policy of civil disobedience, simply rendering to God the things that are God's (Matthew 22:21). The commission to preach the gospel was laid heavily upon Peter by the resurrected Lord and if this brought him into conflict with the authorities, so be it. Like Paul he might have said 'necessity is laid upon me; for woe is unto me if I preach not the gospel ... I have a stewardship entrusted to me' (1 Corinthians 9:16,17). Peter had said to the Lord one day 'Lo, we have left all and have followed Thee', to which He replied that no one who left all behind for His sake, and for the gospel's sake, would ever regret it though it would mean persecutions: eternal life lay ahead. Persecutions would accompany preaching - it was 'the fellowship of His sufferings'.

The murder which was in the mind of the council was tempered by the advice of Gamaliel, and so they contented themselves with beating the apostles before releasing them. Contrary perhaps to expectation they rejoiced that they were counted worthy to suffer dishonour for the Name (v.41). No morbid gratification this, but 'the fellowship of His sufferings'.

Acts 12

'I am ready'. If previously the opposition was inspired by the religious leaders, here it is politically motivated. Herod, to please the Jews who so hated these Christians, kills James and imprisons Peter with a view to slaying him too. But his hour is not yet come. The incident brings the Church to prayer. In God's sovereign will the prison door secured by the authorities and guarded, is opened, only for Peter to face a closed door which should have been readily opened. 'O foolish men, and slow of heart to believe'.

What a lesson this was for the disciples in prayer. The Church was earnest in its prayer for Peter: many of them continued praying at the house, and yet when the answer came there was an unwillingness to believe it. Through Peter's experience God was teaching them an important lesson, and does it not challenge our own attitude in the matter of believing prayer? (Mark 11:24). Do we really believe that God is able to do what we ask, if it is His will?

'The Fellowship of His Sufferings'

It was Paul who penned the words. Peter uses a similar word when he writes about being "partakers of Christ's sufferings" (1 Peter 4:13). To those who so suffer he says 'rejoice', for he anticipates the time of the revelation of His glory. Sufferings and glories - the pattern of the Saviour's experience (1 Peter 1:11). The consideration of the glorious resurrected Christ, raised for our justification and raised that we might not remain in our sins, will lead us into a like experience of suffering and glory. What does it mean?

We shall be ever sensitive to the fact of the Lord's own suffering: the bitterness of the Calvary experience of which Peter writes (1 Peter 3:18). Thank God we have no part in that experience, for there was no sorrow like His sorrow. Can our hearts remain unaffected? This was the culmination of what Peter speaks about in 4:1 "forasmuch then as Christ suffered in the flesh" - He was ever a Man of Sorrows, acquainted with grief, suffering for doing God's will, and it is in this aspect particularly that we can have fellowship in His sufferings. "The disciple is not above his Lord."

Are you ready?

CHAPTER FOURTEEN: THE WIDER VISION

"Brethren ... God made choice among you, that by my mouth the Gentiles should hear the word of the gospel, and believe" (Acts 15:7 RV). God's dealing with the human family altered dramatically with the coming of our Lord Jesus Christ to earth. He came to suffer and die, by means of which death God would call the world to repentance. The message was told first at Jerusalem, but spread "unto the uttermost part of the earth" (Acts 1:8 RV).

The apostle Peter, who on behalf of the disciples made the great confession of Matthew 16:16, "Thou art the Christ, the Son of the living God", subsequently received the keys of the kingdom of heaven. Paul wrote of Peter's work, "He that wrought for Peter unto the apostleship of the circumcision wrought for me also unto the Gentiles" (Galatians 2:8 RV). Peter opened the door of witness at Pentecost, and by the sovereign will and grace of God, it has remained open ever since. However, it was the mind of God that Peter should fulfil the same ministry to the Gentiles. Peter was a strict Jew. For years he had confirmed himself to those of his own race, but he was to learn the purpose of God in calling many from every nation and kindred and people and tongue. He was enlightened in stages. Peter knew that the pleasure-seeking Gentiles would have turned the shores of Galilee into a Roman resort. He knew their way of life and had no doubt resolved never to enter a Gentile house nor eat at a Gentile table. Hence his exclamation when counselled to eat from the contents of the great sheet let down from heaven, "Not so, Lord; for I have never eaten anything that is common and unclean" (Acts 10:14 RV). God led him in stages to change his mind. Consider the following events:

(a) In Acts 6 we read of a disagreement between the Grecian and Hebraic Jews over the apportionment of the daily distribution of food. The matter was resolved by the choice of seven godly men who took responsibility in the matter. We believe the men chosen by the Holy Spirit were Grecian Jews with the exception of Nicolas who was a Gentile proselyte.

(b) In Acts 7, Stephen eloquently testified against the nation of Israel that throughout their entire history they had constantly resisted the work of God's Spirit. Stephen was a Grecian Jew and his words, condemning their total resistance, may have prepared Peter for a door that was being opened for admission of the Gentiles.

(c) During Philip's mission in Acts 8 many Samaritans turned to Christ, believing and being baptized. News of these events reached Jerusalem and brought Peter and John to the scene of revival, among what Jews regarded as a mongrel race and a reproach. Having witnessed at first hand the working of the divine Spirit, both Peter and John returned home, preaching among the Samaritans as they went. God's worldwide purpose was taking shape.

(d) The conversion of Saul of Tarsus was followed closely by his departure into Arabia, but on his return Paul travelled to Jerusalem to stay with Peter for two weeks. Here was a newfound friend and brother whose life had been changed and whose heart had been filled with direct instruction from God. The Lord described him to Ananias as "a chosen vessel unto Me to bear My Name before the Gentiles" (Acts 9:15 RV). Undoubtedly, Peter would have known of this.

(e) As Peter travelled, knowing that "the church throughout all Judea and Galilee and Samaria had peace" (Acts 9:31 RV), he arrived in Joppa where he raised Dorcas. Joppa was on the coast, and as he stood in Simon's house, before him lay the sea of the Gentiles, a world beyond without Christ. What message might have been conveyed to him in such moments we can only speculate, but he was soon to realize the great universal purpose of the gospel that "apart from the Law a righteousness of God hath been manifested" (Romans 3:21 RV).

Leviticus chapter 11 tells us about clean and unclean food according to the ancient law of God for Israel. Peter was well aware of it. Eating only such things as were permitted brought its own distinctiveness from the Gentiles who were regarded as strangers and foreigners, "alienated from the commonwealth of Israel" (Ephesians 2:12 RV). It was clearly necessary that the Levitical distinction should be shown to be irrelevant to the doctrine of the Lord. This was done in a summary and dramatic way, first of all by Peter's vision of the housetop, followed by the conversion of Cornelius, a Roman centurion, and the corroboration of the Holy Spirit (Acts 10:44). This all happened in three days.

The vision that God brought to Peter demonstrated once and for all that the distinction between Jew and Gentile had been abolished in the work of Christ. The grace of God had overflowed to the Gentile nations. Now God united in Peter the matter of vision and duty. Vision without the task to follow can make us dream. The task without the vision makes us routine. We need both. Peter's doubts vanished, however, with the knock on the door by the servants of Cornelius. Subsequently, a party of ten entered Caesarea and, in a changed atmosphere, Peter must have realized he was in the current of divine purpose when he spoke.

Cornelius was an earnest seeker after God. Living north of Joppa, he no doubt came into close touch with the books of the Old Testament and, perhaps under their influence. He was well reported of by the Jews. He had been aroused by what he had heard of the teaching and life of Jesus. He said many prayers, but one in particular, a cry for help, is highlighted in Acts 10:30. A holy angel stood before him, but holy angels are not charged with gospel preaching. Men evangelize the world; God's treasure has been committed to earthen vessels. Philip was in the same city, but this work was not for Philip, Peter had been given the vision of the Gentiles, and Peter brought Cornelius and his friends to Christ at that Spirit-filled gospel meeting. He told the story of Jesus. He gave his personal testimony of the resurrection of the Lord Jesus and proclaimed the forgiveness of sins. There was no talk of circumcision. There was no talk of the Law. The one condition was faith in Jesus Christ.

In the ensuing years, the gospel spread to Galatia, and wherever there is a work of the Lord there is the interest of the Adversary. He was not slow to attack the churches in Galatia, which comprised a mixture of different kinds of people drawn together by the preaching of Paul. Some had been converts from Judaism and others were Greek-speaking Gentiles. Paul would normally have begun his letter to them with a commendation, but when the very essence of the gospel is at stake - 'God's glory and man's salvation' - his uncompromising approach is not surprising.

The Galatians seemed to be in the process of changing their position and disowning the grace of God. A group emerged, unsettling the rest. Initially they had been satisfied with the gospel preached among them by Paul, but subsequently had concluded that this was inadequate: there was the need for Jewish law and tradition. Perhaps some felt insecure with the gospel they had received and believed it should be supplemented with obedience to the Law. In any event, Paul treated the deviation as an emergency. He accused them of turning to an additional gospel which cannot be an alternative gospel. It was a different gospel. It was perceived as 'good news' hut it was not a gospel because it led away from the new birth. It was counterfeit.

According to Galatians 2, Peter was included in the group who met to deal with this issue. They agreed together that the gospel as presented by the Holy Spirit through Paul was the message to be preached. Gentiles were being saved. In fact, Paul had been energized towards the Gentiles and Peter towards the Jews. Of course, James, Peter and John were more remote from the Gentile mission, living in Jerusalem, and when Peter visited Antioch he saw the 'problem' in real life. At first, Peter was perfectly happy to eat with everyone, but when some dissenters arrived from Jerusalem he withdrew, "fearing them that were of the circumcision" (Galatians 2:12 RV). How strange, after God's revelation to him! How powerful the enemy!

Peter was a leading figure, and what leading figures do is noticed. Somehow, he complied with the visitors' consciences instead of instructing them. Race became more important than grace. Instead of a crisis at the conference table it began as a crisis at the dinner table. Peter's behaviour created a false impression. The effect became a flood that caught up the Jewish disciples -

even Barnabas, one of the most attractive men in Scripture. This was not a case of breaking laws. This was a case of failing to walk according to the word of the true gospel. It was a basic subversion, and Paul was shocked. The matter was public and could not be dealt with by a quiet conversation in a corner. A quiet word of correction was inappropriate for a public repudiation of the gospel. Paul rebuked Peter before all the disciples, and Peter recognized, and was pleased, that Paul had intervened to restore the doctrine of the all sufficiency of Christ unto salvation. Such an exercise led to the sublime statement of Paul: "I have been crucified with Christ; yet I live; and yet no longer I, but Christ liveth in me: and that life which I now live in the flesh I live in faith, the faith which is in the Son of God, who loved me, and gave Himself up for me" (Galatians 2:20 RV).

CHAPTER FIFTEEN: PRIESTHOOD AND ELDERHOOD

Peter loved the word 'precious'. In his letters he uses it in different forms, several times. He writes of the 'proof of your faith, being more precious than gold' (1 Peter 1:7). He describes the price of our redemption as the 'precious blood' of Christ (1 Peter 1:19). God's Son is 'precious' (1 Peter 2:4,6). Peter shared an 'equally precious faith', and 'precious and exceeding great promises' (2 Peter 1:1,4). He writes 'for you therefore which believe is the preciousness' (1 Peter 2:7). Peter was also a man who remembered, and, as he wrote his letters, he recalled some of the experiences he had during the time he was with the Lord, as, for example, his reference to having been with Him in 'the holy mount' (2 Peter 1:17,18). How spiritually stimulating would such memories be!

After His resurrection, the Lord Jesus Christ appeared to the apostles "by the space of forty days, and speaking the things concerning the kingdom of God" (Acts 1:3 RV). In his epistles, Peter presents an important aspect of the kingdom of God, that is, the house of God. He shows how the house of God, in this dispensation of grace, is not a building made of materials such as wood, stone, silver and gold, but is a spiritual house composed of believers in the Lord Jesus Christ, that is, those who come to Him as individuals for salvation, and then are built together in obedience and unity to form a collective people for God.

Peter addresses his first letter to believers who were "sojourners of the Dispersion in Pontus, Galatia, Cappadocia, Asia and Bithynia" (1 Peter 1:1 RV), thus showing that the teaching which he and his fellow apostles received from the Lord, and which Peter was now committing to others, was applicable to all those in the churches of God in those provinces. This was to be the practice throughout all the churches of God, the saints in which, in unity together, formed the Fellowship of God's Son, Jesus Christ our Lord (1 Corinthians 1:9). On the night of His betrayal, the Lord prayed to His Father, "Holy Father, keep them in Thy Name ... that they may be one even as we are' (John 17:11 RV). Peter shows how the house of God is the expression of that unity for which the Lord prayed. It is sad that so often among believers, a form of union is substituted for unity, which can be achieved only by following the divine pattern.

The House of God

As Peter writes, he leads his readers along the path of their spiritual experience, sometimes presenting contrasting thoughts to press home the truths he is committing to them. He refers to them as 'living stones' (1 Peter 2:5). They had not always been living stones; once they were dead in trespasses and sins, but they had been redeemed and born again. Taking the metaphor that the apostle uses, we think of how a stone has first to be quarried from a great mass of rock, and such a process demands some form of power. So power is necessary to make a dead sinner a living stone, and we remember that "the gospel is the power of God unto salvation" (Romans 1:16 RV). Only as a sinner yields to the working of the Holy Spirit and comes to the Saviour can he or she be born again, and so become a 'living stone'.

A collection of loose stones does not make a house. For this, two things are necessary; the stones must be shaped and built together, and the architect's plan must be carefully followed. So it is with the house of God. The living stones must come to the Chief Corner Stone, the Lord Himself, and the building must be aligned to that Stone, that is, built in accordance with the will of

God. No deviation can be allowed, just as Moses was instructed concerning the making of the Tabernacle "according to all that I shew thee, the pattern of the dwelling ... even so shall ye make it" (Exodus 25:9 RV Margin). Such is the divine requirement in respect of the present building. As we have noted, the house of God is a spiritual house built of believers. Every believer is a 'living stone', but only those who in obedience come to Christ as Lord are built together to form the house.

A Holy Priesthood

Just as God had a purpose in His house of a past day, He has a purpose with the spiritual house of the present time. Peter tells us that one purpose is for it to function as a holy priesthood (1 Peter 2:5). It is evident that this priesthood is closely associated with the house. The purpose of the holy priesthood is to offer up spiritual sacrifices to God. This is the service of worship of a collective people Godward, and is closely associated with the remembrance of the Lord Jesus Christ in the Breaking of the Bread. God delights to see His people gathered on the Lord's Day to draw near into His presence and to take the bread and wine in remembrance of His beloved Son (Acts 2:42). Being reminded by these symbols of the excellencies of the Lord Jesus Christ, the holy priesthood continues in thanksgiving in the holy place to offer worship and praise to God, in spirit and in truth (John 4:23,24; Hebrews 10:19-22). Every believer is a priest, but not every believer is in the holy priesthood. This collective worship of God is the highest and holiest service that man can offer.

A Royal Priesthood

Another aspect of the collective service of those forming the house of God is that of a royal priesthood (1 Peter 2:9). This involves service manward, and embraces the privilege and responsibility of carrying out to our fellow men and women the message of God's love, so that they too might become 'living stones' and be built into the house of God. In the present age of indifference to the gospel, when so many do not have God in their thoughts, the responsibility of reaching out to unsaved persons is a serious one, but is also a great privilege. Here again, we suggest some association with the Breaking of the Bread which we keep "till He come" (1 Corinthians 11:26 RV). Believers have a glorious prospect ahead, but those who do not know the Saviour 'die in darkness at our side', and, in contrast to the believers' position, are eternally lost. Should we not yearn for them' that they might be saved?

The Elderhood

The people of God forming the house of God are seen by the Lord Jesus Christ as 'the little flock'. The metaphor is an apt one, because as sheep can stray from the flock so can believers fall away from the truth of God. Then, just as a flock of sheep need a shepherd, so there must be shepherds responsible for the care and well-being of the flock of God. In his first letter, Peter refers to the "elders among you" (1 Peter 5:1 RV), and exhorts them to "tend the flock of God which is among you" (1 Peter 5:2 RV). As Peter wrote these words, would he not remember that time when, on the shores of the Sea of Galilee, he heard the risen Lord's thrice repeated question, 'Simon, son of John, lovest thou Me?'. As Peter responded, the threefold exhortation of the Master was "Feed My lambs", "Tend My sheep", "Feed My sheep". Peter was conscious of the approaching end of his days (2 Peter 1:14), and he was anxious that those to whom had been entrusted the care of the saints would be faithful and diligent in their task.

Peter describes these men as 'elders', and then refers to their work as "exercising the oversight" (1 Peter 5:1,2 RV), thus showing that the terms 'elders' and 'overseers' referred to the same body of men, but presenting two different aspects of their work. The word 'elder' can be taken as emphasizing the spiritual maturity and experience of the one so called, while the word 'overseer' views rather the government of the house of God as a unity, and the need to make sure that whatever is done is in accordance with the will of God. Overall we have the thought of the shepherd caring for the saints as we are all exposed to the wiles of the evil one.

There were elders (plural) in each church of God, and there is no thought in Scripture of a presiding elder having the sole rule of an assembly. Peter writes, 'the elders among you I exhort'. As we have noted, Peter's letter is addressed to the churches of God in the five Roman provinces, and just as they are seen as one flock, so the elders among them are seen as one elderhood. This unity of the elderhood is demonstrated clearly in Acts 15. Peter was present on that occasion (Acts 15:6), and related his experiences at Joppa and at Caesarea with Cornelius. Other elders present took part in the discussion, and the conclusions reached by the elders together were sent to the churches (Acts 15:23; 16:4).

Peter Looks Forward

We have thought of Peter as a man who remembered, but he also looked forward. He writes of "an inheritance incorruptible and undefiled, and that fadeth not away, reserved in heaven for you" (1 Peter 1:4,5 RV). While he recalled with joy those days he spent with his beloved Lord, he treasured the promises relating to the future. He valued the teaching he had received. They were truths for his day, and they are for our day too. May we value the teaching of Scripture about the unity of the house of God and its functions, and consider it as God considers it, precious.

CHAPTER SIXTEEN: SPIRITUAL GROWTH

When Peter was moved to write his first epistle he wrote to the 'elect' and reminded them that their election had been 'unto obedience and sprinkling of the blood of Jesus Christ' and his second letter was addressed to the same people. By referring to them as 'elect' he was calling their attention to their position as an elect race (2:9) and by referring them back to the blood of sprinkling in Exodus 24:3 he was reminding them of the obedience that the people of Israel had confessed at Sinai when they said, 'All the words which the Lord hath spoken will we do and be obedient'.

In Ephesians 1, Paul had written to those who had been chosen 'in Him before the foundation of the world'. That choosing had been to salvation which could not be made more sure than it was; being based upon the work of the Lord Jesus and which did not need the works of man, either to bring it about or to supplement it. In his second epistle (1:10) Peter urges them to make their calling and election sure. What therefore is that election? Surely it is their election to the service of God. That is the election that is to be made more sure. To effect this spiritual growth was necessary, and Peter touches upon this growth in several ways in his epistle, calling upon his own experiences to underline it.

The apostle Paul had in his epistles shown how spiritual growth could be attained, but Peter develops the theme in his own inimitable way. He reminds his readers that the salvation they enjoyed had been written about by the prophets of old who had not experienced it for themselves, but had diligently searched the scriptures they were writing to see the hidden meaning behind the words of the Spirit. Moreover, even the angels in heaven, created and sinless beings, desired to look into these things.

'Wherefore', says Peter, 'gird up the loins of your mind'. There is much to be learned from that word 'Wherefore'. Just consider all that has been said before. Remember you are the heirs to the promises that the prophets had written about, but had not been fulfilled. Remember that even angelic beings would like to know more about the things that you are privileged to know. Taking all the foregoing into account, says Peter, gird up your loins. The girding up of the loins signifies that the workman was about to undertake his task. He did not gird up his loins if he was about to take his rest. Peter had known what it was to gird his loins when he was fishing although there was one occasion when he had been naked whilst about his work (John 21:7). He also remembered that on the last night together, the Lord had girded Himself. That time it was with a towel so that he could wash the disciples' feet.

As recorded in John 21:18 the Lord had told Peter that when he was young he girded himself, but when he became old others would gird him and he would be taken where he would prefer not to go. Peter also remembered that Herod had taken him and Put him in prison with the execution fixed for the next day, but God had sent His angel who had said, "Gird yourself" (Acts 12:8). He had been taken into prison where he would have preferred not to go and now the angel was taking him out. It would have been quite within the powers of the angel to gird Peter, but no, he was to gird himself for his release. Now he says to his readers, 'Gird yourselves'. There is work to be done to attain spiritual growth. You will not get it by taking things easily, assuming that it will come of its own volition.

We are not to fashion ourselves according to our former lusts (1:14). Here Peter was echoing the words of Paul in Romans 12. Our outward appearance should be in accordance with our inward new-born nature and we should be holy in all manner of living. Knowing this, says Peter, "ye were redeemed from your vain manner of life by the precious blood of a Lamb without blemish". He remembered the blood of the lamb without blemish that he and the Lord had partaken of on the last night before the Cross. That had been a lamb without blemish as far as men could see, but the next day he had seen a Lamb slain at the Cross that was without blemish not only as far as the eye of man was concerned, but was without blemish in the sight of the all-seeing God.

'Ye shall be holy' (1:16 RV). This is but one of many references to the Old Testament. He was quoting from Leviticus 11:44 where God was commanding physical holiness upon His people. Peter is calling to a spiritual holiness and a longing for the spiritual milk (2:2) which would have both a negative and a positive effect. Negatively we are to put off all guile, and positively we are to put on the new man (Ephesians 4:24). Growing unto salvation is a positive and continuing thing. We are to abstain from fleshly lusts (2:11) that the Gentiles "may by your goods works ... glorify God in the day of visitation". This seems to refer to a day when God will visit the Gentiles either in mercy (Luke 19:44) or in judgement (Isaiah 10:3). Either way glory will be given to God.

The good works of the believer may be referred to in Luke 16, and Peter would have remembered the parable where the Lord commends to His disciples that they make to themselves friends by means of the mammon of unrighteousness. Is this not a call to us to use our money (mammon) by such means that the Gentiles may be saved thereby? No salvation can be bought by money itself. The world does not contain sufficient wealth to save even one sinner. But our money can be used for the printing of leaflets that can be used to bring salvation. It can be used to finance the work of the Lord's evangelists and others to go out into all the world and preach the gospel. Surely God will be glorified by this means. Who knows how many will welcome us when we reach the heavenly tabernacles, grateful that we used our wealth, such as it was, to finance the preaching of the gospel by which they were saved? Not that this absolves us of our responsibility to preach.

Peter also commends his readers to follow His steps (2:21). Note that he does not say follow in His steps? That would be an impossible task for a sinful people to follow in the steps of a sinless Master. There had been a day when Peter had stepped out of the boat to walk to his Master on the water. Sadly he ceased (metaphorically) to follow His steps and sank. Let us follow His steps, says Peter, and learn to live thereby. 'Finally', says Peter in chapter 3, verse 8. That is another word which throws us back on all that has gone before. The epistle is not a collection of unconnected threads but is a seamless robe. We are not to return reviling upon those who revile us. The Lord reviled not back: (2:23). Take a look at the English word 'reviled' and spell it backwards and we get the word 'deliver'. True it is that He reviled not back but delivered instead all who through their lifetime were subject to bondage. Peter again refers to the Old Testament, this time to Psalm 34 (vv. 13,14). This Psalm bad been written by David when he was in the land of the Philistines and realized that he would not attain to God's promises by reviling the Lord's anointed. He had got himself into a precarious position by accepting the hospitality of a Philistine king and in order to extricate himself he had feigned madness. Are we extricating ourselves from the grip of the world or are we adopting its methods in order to promote our well-being?

Beginning his second letter Peter says "we have obtained a like precious faith". The word obtained here means "having obtained by lot". The faith that we have obtained has been allotted to us by divine grace - an act independent of human control. In the same way the children of Israel had obtained their inheritance (Joshua chapter 14). They lived on the land that had been given them by lot and so must we. Our faith has been allotted to us for the same reason - that we might live by faith thereby. "The just shall live by (or out of) faith" because that faith rests in the righteousness of our God and Saviour Jesus Christ - true testimony to the deity of our Lord Jesus.

CHAPTER SEVENTEEN: THE PROMISE OF HIS COMING

Have you ever received an unexpected letter from far away during a particularly difficult time, and your spirits have been lifted by it because the writer so obviously understands what you are going through?

A Very Visible Minority

The Jewish Christians living in Northern Turkey in the first century were certainly living in very difficult times of open persecution. All around them were orthodox Jews and Gentiles: the Jews were committed to eliminating them as a 'sect', and the Gentiles believed strongly in their numerous Roman and Greek gods and goddesses. Paul had encountered hostility in his travels there, but they were living in it every day. These were the days of Emperor Nero, who had already expelled all the Christians from Rome. 'Suffering as a Christian' was a very real thing for them.

And so Peter the apostle, far away, decides to write to them - not once but twice. His time to help them was getting short. The Lord had shown him that he would soon die. But instead of being preoccupied with that, his heart went out to those who also had received 'like precious faith'. Previously the Lord Jesus had told him 'by what death he would glorify God' (John 21:19). Peter had said he was ready to go into death with the Lord Jesus at the time of His crucifixion; that was not the will of God, but now this glorious death approached. He must hurry to convey to those dear kindred souls in the five northern provinces the word of encouragement they needed.

What Would Encourage Them?

But how to do it? Anything he could tell them they already knew. It wasn't information they needed. They needed what we all need when troubles surround us - someone to remind us of what we already know, to put it all back into perspective, to help us to lift up our eyes and see things as they really are. And, as a result, to be stirred - stirred into action and resolve. And so he begins.

He reminds them of the holy calling that they had received from God, that they had been selected by Him from all the people in the world to be His obedient ones, to be His new covenant people for divine service. He reminds them of the example of Christ's own suffering in the flesh (which Peter had seen first-hand). He reminds them that their present suffering would not go on indefinitely, how God regards their steadfastness through it all, and that they were not alone, others were linked with them.

And finally, and perhaps greatest of all, he reminds them of 'the promise of His coming'. He calls it their 'living hope' - the hope that stays alive within them - of the full and glorious revelation of the Lord Jesus, whom the world could not now see by faith and would not acknowledge. It was the hope of the fulfilment of their salvation, not just of bodily resurrection, but of their soul, their whole person, which was being preserved by the Lord Jesus for that day. It was the hope of finally receiving their eternal inheritance. That inheritance was safely reserved in heaven for them; and they were being preserved on earth for it. And so he helps them to anticipate in their minds the unsurpassed joy that both they and the Lord would have at that future day, when He would present them faultless before the presence of His glory with exceeding joy (Jude 24).

The Prophetic Word

The knowledge of the future coming of the Lord comes from the prophetic scriptures. Peter describes these scriptures as a light of truth shining in a world where there is only darkness. It begins to emerge within us, initially just faintly, until it brightens within our hearts as we pay attention to it until it reaches full assurance. This is divine revelation from the Word. Proverbs 20:27 tells us that the spirit of a man is the lamp of the Lord, and it is through our spirit that the Spirit of God brings us insight and conviction regarding the Scriptures. Peter had seen the glory of the Lord Jesus with his eyes on the mount of Transfiguration. But it was through this inner revelation that Peter had come to the conviction that Jesus was 'the Christ, the Son of the, living God' (Matthew 16:16). This inner revelation of the prophetic word, he says, is more sure.

Faith and Hope

In complete contrast to the ungodliness and falseness of those among whom they were living, Peter appeals to these dear saints to be mindful of these sure things. It is the Scriptures that give us hope, if they are combined with the faith on our part that gives us the assurance of the things hoped for (Hebrews 11:1). Because of this hope they would actually be hastening (the Revised Version: earnestly desiring) the coming glorious revelation of Christ and vindication from their enemies; they would long for it to come sooner. Perhaps nothing makes us want the return of the Lord to come soon more than troubles here; perhaps that is one of the reasons we are given such troubles.

Meanwhile, the other ingredient, their faith, was being sorely tried. No doubt they were praying continually for relief. Why was God not giving it? But with every passing day of faithful endurance they were enhancing the praise and honour and glory that they would receive from the Lord Himself in that day, as their faith was being proven.

The Day of the Lord

But the coming of the Lord Jesus has another side. To the believer, it should be all joy - the end of suffering, full salvation, receiving our inheritance. But what to the ungodly who were the cause of all their present distress? And so, in his final chapter, Peter goes into some detail about the judgement that will come to the world with the future revelation of the Lord Jesus. It is the time referred to as 'the day of the Lord', which follows the rapture of believers at 'the day of Christ'. The day of the Lord will be a fearsome time for the ungodly. It includes the great tribulation, the spectacular return of the Lord with His saints to the earth, His millennial (thousand-year) reign, and the final judgement at the great white throne, at which those not found written in the Lamb's book of life and fallen angels will be delivered into the lake of fire. It culminates in the destruction of this heaven and cursed earth with great fire, explosive noise and fervent heat and its replacement with a new, spotless, heaven and earth.

Now, to the unbeliever, all this is incredible and foolish. Peter tells his readers that one of the ways they can know that these are the last days is that there will be many sceptics, many who will ridicule the idea of the coming of the Lord, and who do not let it interfere with their self-indulgent lives. It is very reminiscent of those who were living at the arrival of the flood that Noah told them was coming. They were eating and drinking, marrying and living in blissful ignorance of the impending judgement. Peter uses the event of that flood to make his point that God does intervene in the affairs of this world.

'All things continue as they were from the beginning of the creation' is the conventional scientific explanation of things; nothing is changing and so nothing will. But it is God Himself who makes and maintains those natural processes, and God can and does overturn them to serve His purpose. It is significant that Peter says that these people wilfully forget what happened at the time of the flood. God had separated water at the time of creation, reserving it for use in Noah's day. Similarly, there is fire reserved today that will be used for the destruction of this present evil world and the works of ungodly men. The future judgement of the ungodly is inevitable. It is a serious, serious thing to wilfully set aside the Word of God.

God's Timing and Ours

How easy it is for us to misunderstand the ways of God. What to Him are the two thousand years since Christ's ascension to heaven? They are like two short days. God's sense of timing and ours are so different. God isn't tardy, He is long-suffering. What a mistake to interpret inaction by God as any inability or unwillingness on His part. The day of the Lord will come at a time when men are asleep and feeling secure, like a thief comes, and then it will be too late for them. But for us, it will be our entering into the glory of our inheritance with Him.

As those dear saints read Peter's letters to them, how it must in fact have stirred them up. Their hearts were pure before God and Peter's final act of ministry to them as an apostle and servant of Jesus Christ would help them through to the end. Peter knew so much of the ups and downs of a life spent following the Lord Jesus - often discouragements and mistakes, but surely never any lack of zeal, and never defeat. And so he encourages them in the light of all he has brought again to their memory: what manner of persons ought you to be, in holy conduct and godliness.

ABOUT THE AUTHORS

CHAPTER ONE: PHIL CAPEWELL

CHAPTER TWO: JAMES MARTIN

CHAPTER THREE: JOHN KERR

CHAPTER FOUR: GREG NEELY

CHAPTER FIVE: JOHN MILLER

CHAPTER SIX: ROY DICKSON

CHAPTER SEVEN: MARTIN DYER

CHAPTER EIGHT: IAIN HUNTER

CHAPTER NINE: ALAN SANDS

CHAPTER TEN: JOHN DRAIN

CHAPTER ELEVEN: PHIL CAPEWELL

CHAPTER TWELVE: MICHAEL ELLIOTT

CHAPTER THIRTEEN: LEONARD ROSS

CHAPTER FOURTEEN: ROBERT SHAW

CHAPTER FIFTEEN: RON HICKLING

CHAPTER SIXTEEN: KEN RILEY

CHAPTER SEVENTEEN: KEITH DORRICOTT

Did you love *Fisherman to Follower: The Life and Teaching of Simon Peter*? Then you should read *Collected Writings On ... The Cross of Christ* by Hayes Press!

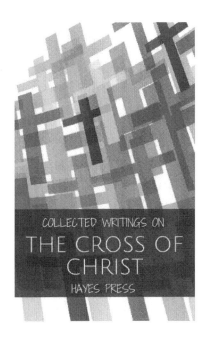

This book takes a detailed look at the significance and ramifications of the most important event in human history - the crucifixion of Jesus Christ.

CHAPTER ONE: CURSED ... ON THE TREE
CHAPTER TWO: STANDING BY THE CROSS
CHAPTER THREE: THE BLOOD OF HIS CROSS
CHAPTER FOUR: THE WORD OF THE CROSS
CHAPTER FIVE: LET HIM DENY HIMSELF
CHAPTER SIX: REDEEMED AT THE CROSS
CHAPTER SEVEN: THE WAY OF THE CROSS

CHAPTER EIGHT: JESUS' WORDS ON THE CROSS
CHAPTER NINE: CALVARY NAILS
CHAPTER TEN: THE CROSS FORETOLD - THE LAMB SLAIN
CHAPTER ELEVEN: THE CROSS FORETOLD - ALL THAT THE PROPHETS HAVE SPOKEN
CHAPTER TWELVE: THE CROSS FORETOLD - IN ALL THE SCRIPTURES
CHAPTER THIRTEEN: THE CROSS FORETOLD - NOW IS MY SOUL TROUBLED
CHAPTER FOURTEEN: THE CROSS - CRUCIFIED IN WEAKNESS

A short bonus book on the Beatitudes - Upside Down Values - is also included.

Also by Hayes Press

The Road Through Calvary: 40 Devotional Readings
Lovers of God's House
Different Discipleship: Jesus' Sermon on the Mount
The House of God: Past, Present and Future
The Kingdom of God
Knowing God: His Names and Nature
Needed Truth 1888-1988: A Centenary Review of Major Themes
Churches of God: Their Constitution and Functions
Collected Writings On ... Exploring Biblical Fellowship
Collected Writings On ... Exploring Biblical Hope
Collected Writings On ... The Cross of Christ
Builders for God
Collected Writings On ... Exploring Biblical Faithfulness
Collected Writings On ... Exploring Biblical Joy
Possessing the Land: Spiritual Lessons from Joshua
Collected Writings On ... Exploring Biblical Holiness
Collected Writings On ... Exploring Biblical Faith
Collected Writings On ... Exploring Biblical Love
These Three Remain...Exploring Biblical Faith, Hope and Love
The Teaching and Testimony of the Apostles
Pressure Points - Biblical Advice for 20 of Life's Biggest Challenges
The Exalted One - 12 Portraits of Christ
The Faith: Outlines of Scripture Doctrine
Elders and the Elderhood: In Principle, In Practice
Key Doctrines of the Christian Gospel
Is There a Purpose to Life?
Bible Covenants 101

The Hidden Christ: Offerings and Sacrifices
The Hidden Christ Volume 1: Types and Shadows in the Old Testament
Fisherman to Follower: The Life and Teaching of Simon Peter

About the Publisher

Hayes Press (www.hayespress.org) is a registered charity in the United Kingdom, whose primary mission is to disseminate the Word of God, mainly through literature. It is one of the largest distributors of gospel tracts and leaflets in the United Kingdom, with over 100 titles and hundreds of thousands despatched annually.

Hayes Press also publishes Plus Eagles Wings, a fun and educational Bible magazine for children, six times a year and Golden Bells, a popular daily Bible reading calendar in wall or desk formats.

Also available are over 100 Bibles in many different versions, shapes and sizes, Christmas cards, Christian jewellery, Eikos Bible Art, Bible text posters and much more!

Made in the USA
Middletown, DE
28 February 2018